ULTIMATE REALITY

Ultimate Reality:

A CHALLENGE TO THE MATERIALIST PARADIGM

Rodger Paul Shute, MA

Where do we come from? What are we? Where do we go?

Published by Romar Philosophical Publishing LLC.

ISBN: 978-1-7358168-0-7

Contents

Acknowledgment

THIS BOOK IS DEDICATED TO my wife and soul mate, Margo. For over forty-eight years, she has believed in me and encouraged me on my quest to understand the mystery of our existence and the nature of ultimate reality. By her example, she has been the most important teacher in my search for the meaning of life.

Foreword

IN THE MUSEUM OF FINE Arts in Boston, there hangs a painting by French post-Impressionist artist Eugène Henri Paul Gauguin. In the upper left-hand corner of the painting, there is an inscription that asks *"D'où Venons Nous / Que Sommes Nous / Où Allons Nous,"* which translates to "Where do we come from / What are we / Where do we go." There are no question marks, commas, or dashes. All the words are capitalized.[1] The painting is said to be a contemplation of life and death, which could be discerned from the subjects in the painting. Gauguin's questions have plagued thinkers since prehistory.

The first part of the inscription, "Where do we come from," is explored in the chapter on evolution. The second question, "What are we," is addressed in the chapter on consciousness. The third question, "Where do we go," is the subject of the last chapter on the continuation of consciousness.

For Gauguin, life only had meaning if you exercised your will to achieve what you were meant to achieve. For him that meant abandoning his wife and children to become the painter he was sure he could be. Most of us would find that path to finding meaning extreme.

By pondering Gaugin's questions, we may not find the answers—perhaps we are not meant to find them—but the search can bring us to understand how deep the mystery of existence goes. We can begin our search by opening our minds to new ideas and by recognizing the beauty and wonder of the world around us. The recognition that there is a hidden dimension to reality can help us gain a confidence that life does have meaning. The realization that there is a hidden, divine, sacred, ultimate reality bestows upon us a sense of awe and wonder, and it is that experience which carries with it the knowledge that life is meaningful. It is our job to find what that meaning is for us.

One problem we find when searching for evidence of this reality is language. Werner Heisenberg, an early contributor to quantum theory, recognized this problem:

> What we are observing is not nature itself, but nature exposed to our method of questioning. And how do we question? All of our methods of interrogating nature depend on language—and it is the very nature of language to refer to things. We therefore think in terms of things. How can we possibly think of non-things, nothings, nothing?[2]

Buddhism, along with some mystery religions, sees the cause of unhappiness and suffering as ignorance of the true nature of reality. Seeking to recognize and understand the divine attributes of ultimate reality is a meaningful path to lasting happiness and fulfillment.

Chapter 1 discusses the importance of being open minded. "Overcertainty" in our beliefs causes us to mistake our beliefs for knowledge. There is very little outside of mathematics that can be known with certainty. We often go to great lengths to protect what we believe rather than consider views that are in conflict with those beliefs. We should be open minded to the beliefs and opinions of others, while remaining skeptical in the true sense of the word. This means not being gullible or excessively wary.[3] Many of the thinkers cited in this book have dared to question the materialist paradigm, and for that, some have paid a price. However, the greater the antipathy expressed toward such daring scientists, and the more vocal the ad hominem attacks, the more I have come to suspect that those scientists are closing in on something valuable.

The distinction between believing something and knowing something is important: confusing belief with knowledge can cause a person to categorically dismiss an idea without investigating whether the idea has merit. This is a problem that plagues our society in subtle ways and in every area of discourse, from religion to politics. The inability to consider the merit in another person's idea or point of view often leads to both parties becoming even more intransigent in their views. When this happens between individuals, violence can result; when it happens between nations, the violence can become catastrophic. The resistance to the ideas presented in this book often takes the form of ad hominem attacks or worse. Failure to discuss the merits of an idea, no matter how far outside mainstream thinking, is inexcusable. We should all seek to walk the fine line between gullibility and complete skepticism.

Chapter 2 explores the evidence for an ultimate reality that manifests in our day-to-day objective world and provides clues in psychology, physics, and biology. The work of others, upon which I base my discussion, has impeccable credentials; years have been spent investigating the topics upon which they are writing. The evidence presented convincingly shows that reality consists not only of what we can perceive through our five senses, but an equally real, unperceived dimension, which influences our objective world.

There are many different names for this ultimate reality: akashic field, morphic field, holographic field, multiverse, nirvana, and so on. However, the idea that there is but one reality with many different attributes is more parsimonious and is therefore to be preferred *if* it can account for all the relevant facts. Huxley felt similarly. In his book *The Perennial Philosophy*, he quotes Buddhist sage Yung-chia Ta-Shih: "One Reality, all-comprehensive, contains within itself all realities."[4]

The hidden aspect of the one reality is not something new. It has been known and written about since ancient times. Since the discoveries of quantum physics, however, some physicists have dared to recognize that our description of reality is incomplete without considering a spiritual dimension. Nevertheless, mainstream science still resists considering the anomalous features of quantum physics such as entanglement and complementarity as evidence of a nonmaterial dimension.

Chapter 3 discusses causality, coincidence, seriality, serendipity, and synchronicity. These words, often used interchangeably, differ from one another in meaning. Eastern and Western views of the connections between events also differ. Understanding how other cultures view causality can help us make sense of the universal interconnectedness of quantum theory.

Chapter 4 investigates theories of evolution, noting the problems with the Darwinian–neo-Darwinian rubric. The meaning of the word "evolution" is explored, along with its application to cosmology and biology. The theories of intelligent design, teleology, Lamarckism, and the problem of forms are discussed. Somewhat surprisingly, the most vocal advocates of Darwin's theories ignore some of the doubts that even Darwin himself had concerning his theories. I posit that perhaps the theories of intelligent design and Darwinian evolution are not as antithetical as they appear if one considers the role of time.

Chapter 5 explores consciousness. The nature of consciousness is not susceptible to analysis by materialist science. Attempts to define consciousness are explored, as well as the theory of its ubiquity. Two major theories of consciousness, emergentism and panpsychism, are compared. The techniques used to determine whether something is conscious are discussed. Some theorists argue that even subatomic particles exhibit behavior that might be termed "conscious." The problem of speciesism, a form of discrimination based upon species membership, is examined.

There is no unanimity about the nature of consciousness among scientists and philosophers. Some refuse to even consider the possibility that nonhuman animals, and even plants, may exhibit rudimentary forms of consciousness or intelligence, even if we accept definitions for those terms that apply to human behavior.

Chapter 6 investigates how altered states of consciousness may allow us to experience the ultimate reality. Those altered states of consciousness include gratuitous experiences of the sacred,[5] religious experiences, meditation, dreams, entheogens, out-of-body experiences, near-death experiences (NDEs), and hypnosis.

Altered states of consciousness allow the individual an opportunity to experience the ultimate reality behind the doors of perception. An experience related by Emerson is given as an example of a gratuitous experience of the sacred. Religious experiences are contrasted with mystical experiences. Meditation's ability to provide a glimpse of the hidden reality is described. Dreams are doorways to the hidden realm, and they cause us to question the distinction between subjective and objective reality. Stephen LaBerge of the Stanford Sleep Research Center suspects that the possibility that, in at least some circumstances, the world we experience when we dream may be objective to some degree.[6] There is a question as to why we rush to characterize an experience as objective or subjective, real or unreal. These are words we created that seek to distinguish between experiences in a consensual reality from those in a nonconsensual reality; such distinctions ignore the fact that to the experiencer, whether the experience is objective or subjective, is not as important as the fact of the experience itself.

Chapter 7 discusses death and transcendence, and what transcendence might mean to the individual. The mystery of what may survive is discussed. The questionable use of regression hypnosis to recall prior lives is critically examined. If one assumes reincarnation to be a fact, that leaves the question of what the state of existence is in the intermediate period between death and rebirth. The bardo of *The Tibetan Book of the Dead*, and reports of individuals who have undergone regression hypnosis, describe similar states of existence. The reports of individuals who have attempted to contact the dead through "mediums" or mirrors are also discussed.

The possibility of rebirth is explored, with consideration given to both Buddhist philosophy and Hindu religion. The idea of reincarnation necessarily requires a deeper understanding of exactly what it is that is said to reincarnate, including the philosophical and psychological issues concerning the nature of the Self.

1

Belief and Truth

The discovery of truth is prevented more effectively, not by the false appearance of things present and which mislead into error, not directly by weakness of the reasoning powers, but by preconceived opinion, by prejudice.
—Arthur Schopenhauer

The solution of great problems requires the giving up of great prejudices.
—Paul Dirac, Nobel Prize–winning physicist (1902–1984)

At its simplest and most direct, tabooism is manifested as derision and rejection by scientists (and non-scientists) of those new discoveries or new inventions that cannot be fitted into the existing framework of knowledge.
—Richard Milton, science writer

The search for truth is more precious than its possession.
—Albert Einstein

Everything we hear is an opinion, not a fact. Everything we see is a perspective, not the truth.
—Marcus Aurelius

Those who don't believe in magic will never find it.
—Roald Dahl

[W]e never disbelieve anything except for the reason that we believe something else which contradicts the first thing.
—William James

MANY OF THE PROBLEMS FACING our intellectually inhospitable world are due in large part to individuals, institutions, and nations holding firm to their beliefs and their unwillingness to consider any ideas in conflict with those beliefs. This rigidity in beliefs is what I prefer to call "overcertainty," which, if it is not a word, should be. There is very little, outside of mathematics, that can be known with certainty. Most of what we claim to know is merely what we have chosen to believe, either consciously or unconsciously. An unfortunate negative consequence of overcertainty is that we stop gathering information that could challenge or threaten our beliefs. We often seek to protect and reinforce our beliefs because that is more comforting and less threatening to us. When our minds hold conflicting information, we experience "cognitive dissonance," a term based upon a theory developed by social psychologist Leon Festinger.[7]

I suggest that most people consider belief and faith to have the same meaning, and perhaps they do. A dictionary definition tells us that faith can be thought of as a confident belief in the truth, value, or trustworthiness of a person, idea, or thing, whereas a belief is not based upon logical proof or material evidence. Belief may be thought of as a mental act of trusting or placing confidence in a person or thing: a mental acceptance of or conviction in the truth or actuality of something.[8] The real confusion lies in the difference between belief and knowledge, and this confusion can cause major problems, some of which can have serious repercussions. Problems with intractable beliefs, sometimes witnessed in religious and political intolerance, can only be resolved when both parties are able to accept the fact that their beliefs do not constitute knowledge and thereby come to understand and accept that others may have beliefs that are equally defensible.

It is my objective that some of the subjects discussed in this book challenge your beliefs. It is not, however, my objective to change your beliefs or have you accept any of the ideas presented here on faith. What I hope to do is expose you to the work of knowledgeable theorists whose ideas lie outside of the materialist paradigm, a paradigm that considers everything, including consciousness, to consist solely of matter and interactions of matter. The reluctance to consider new ideas is often deeply rooted in our own psychological makeup, but not everyone suffers equally. Some individuals may be too gullible; others are too wary. Fortunately, there are many open-minded men and women with whom dispassionate discourse can occur, and who are open to consider evidence in support of new ideas that might have the effect of causing them to change their minds. Unfortunately, it is often those in power who control the flow of ideas to prestigious journals and thus access to research funding. Protective of their own "turf," they are not always receptive to new ideas, and in some cases they may even become hostile.[9]

As I said, we form our beliefs due, in part, to our psychological makeup. This receptiveness to new ideas is influenced by several factors:

- *Gullibility.* In common usage this might mean that we are overly receptive to a new idea; we may be easily duped or deceived. In other words, one believes what one has heard indiscriminately.

- *Excessive wariness or denial.* Excessive wariness connotes reluctance or refusal to believe; we may not only resist a new idea that is well founded, but no matter how solid the evidence, we may actually disbelieve it.

- *Skepticism.* Skepticism is the state of mind that involves keeping an open mind with regard to new information; we continue to question and examine, but we do not take a position of "belief" or "disbelief."

It is easy to understand why gullibility is problematic. If one is not the least bit selective as to what they accept as a belief, they become easy prey for people with harmful intent. Excessive wariness can also be problematic. Refusing to consider a new idea is one manifestation of excessive wariness; another is when you form a "disbelief" in the new idea. For example, if someone tells you they have seen a UFO (unidentified flying object), you may accept that as a fact without further thought (gullibility), or you may insist that they are lying, firmly disbelieving them that there is such a phenomenon (excessive wariness). Alternatively, you may find it interesting and continue to gather information about the alleged experience in particular, and the UFO phenomenon in general (skepticism). Generally, you should not feel an immediate need to believe a statement or doubt the claim being made. However, if you are asked or compelled to take some action based on the claim, you should investigate further and adjust your belief or disbelief accordingly.

Many individuals probably confuse the state of excessive wariness with skepticism, even though the two terms have very little in common. The word "skeptic" comes from the Greek word *skeptikoi*, which referred to those philosophers who refused to take dogmatic positions, but rather claimed to be always engaged in "investigation" or "consideration" (*skepsis*) of questions.[10] Clearly, contrary to its popular usage, it does not mean "disbelief." In other words, skepticism implies inquiring, rather than forming a belief or disbelief. After one has performed an inquiry, they may have reasons to form a belief or disbelief (such as the need to take action of some kind), at which time they cease to be a skeptic.

The famous astronomer Carl Sagan recognized the need for balance in a lecture he gave in Pasadena in 1987, although there, too, he is guilty of misusing the historical meaning of the term "skeptical," which he conflates with a closed mind:

> It seems to me what is called for is an exquisite balance between two conflicting needs: the most skeptical scrutiny of all hypotheses that are served up to us and at the same time a great openness to new ideas. If you are only skeptical, then no new

ideas make it through to you. You never learn anything new. You become a crotchety old person convinced that nonsense is ruling the world. (There is, of course, much data to support you.) On the other hand, if you are open to the point of gullibility and have not an ounce of skeptical sense in you, then you cannot distinguish useful ideas from the worthless ones. If all ideas have equal validity then you are lost, because then, it seems to me, no ideas have any validity at all.[11]

I suggest that becoming a true "skeptic," in the original Greek meaning of the word, should be everyone's goal. We should all continue to question ideas presented to us (no matter the source), but should guard against being too quick to believe or disbelieve. By putting off forming a belief or disbelief for as long as possible, we continue to gather information, which facilitates better decision-making. In learning to loosen our adherence to beliefs that are not essential to the actions we must take in our daily lives, the world can transform into a magical place that presents us with awe and wonder. The more we acknowledge and recognize the beauty and mystery of creation, the less we will find ourselves burdened by trivial cares and concerns.

Absent a requirement to take some kind of action, it can behoove us to be skeptics in the true sense of the word. The longer we are able to continue assimilating information without having formed a belief or disbelief, the better decision makers we will become. The quote from James at the beginning of this chapter bears repeating: "We never disbelieve anything except for the reason that we believe something else which contradicts the first thing."[12] By recognizing our biases and working to keep them from preventing the consideration of new ideas, we may learn new information that can help us make better decisions. This is not a suggestion that one should practice the kind of skepticism described by Sagan. Such skepticism could cause one to become too passive, rendering them unable to make any decisions.[13]

With respect to the benefits of deferring believing or disbelieving, Krishnamurti, a respected Indian philosopher, offered his views in his book *Think on These Things*:

> If you hold firmly to some set of beliefs or other, you look at everything through that particular prejudice or tradition; you don't have any contact with reality…And when you observe something for the first time, what happens? You automatically translate what you are seeing according to your prejudices, don't you? You experience it according to your conditioning as a communist, a socialist, a capitalist, or some other "ist." Whereas, if you are none of these things and therefore do not look through the screen of any idea or belief, but actually have the direct contact, then you will notice what an extraordinary relationship there is between you and what you observe. If you have no prejudice, no bias, if you are open, then everything around you becomes extraordinarily interesting, tremendously alive.[14]

Krishnamurti's observations help us to understand the problems that come about by maintaining a rigid mindset against considering new ideas. When new information conflicts with a belief you hold, you experience Festinger's "cognitive dissonance." This may cause you to accept other beliefs simply because they are in accord with beliefs you hold, without giving them any deliberate consideration.

For example, atheists are often supportive of Darwinian evolution because intelligent design theory is inconsistent with their atheism. Conversely, a Christian might have trouble with Darwinian theory because it connotes the absence of a divine influence in evolution. To reduce this dissonance, they will move to eliminate this conflict. In this case, they are confronted with two inconsistent cognitions (i.e., bits of information that are in conflict with one another). Other tools that help to reduce conflict include blaming, denying, or criticizing.[15]

Individuals vary in the degree of cognitive dissonance they experience when confronting ideas that conflict with their beliefs, depending on the degree to which they cling to those beliefs. Festinger acknowledged that there is a variation in "tolerance for dissonance." For some, he claimed, dissonance is extremely painful and intolerable, while others can accept a greater degree of dissonance without feeling uncomfortable.[16] Examples of cognitive dissonance and the actions that result from them are common. If an individual is a smoker, they may rationalize their actions by trivializing the medical evidence that links smoking to lung cancer, or by arguing that they are likely to die of something else first. Another example might be an individual who desires to attain a goal but is unable to do so. In that event, they may reduce the dissonance they are experiencing by arguing they didn't really want the goal or by criticizing those who *do* achieve it as unworthy (an example of the "sour grapes" moral in the Aesop fable).[17]

Some individuals, confronted with ideas that are in opposition to beliefs in which they have a significant investment of time, treasure, or emotion, will cling to their beliefs ever more strongly, even in cases where doing so becomes indefensible. Consider the example of Lord Kelvin, a physicist and natural philosopher, who made major contributions in the field of thermodynamics. Kelvin introduced the concept of absolute zero and the Kelvin temperature scale based upon it. However, he too showed intolerance to new ideas when he renounced Röntgen's discovery of x-rays as a hoax. He also steadfastly denied that helium could be produced from radium (a major discovery of Ramsay and Soddy) until the day he died.[18] Dirac's observation that "[t]he solution of great problems requires giving up of great prejudices" is often easier said than done—even for great minds such as that of Lord Kelvin.[19]

When we form a belief, we should recognize it as a belief, not knowledge. It is important to make a distinction between the two, for you can *believe* something that is not true; however, if you *know* something, then it cannot be false. This criterion can be helpful when evaluating an idea someone holds as a belief. If that belief *could* be false, even if it is only remotely possible that it could be false, then it fails to qualify as knowledge. If we can accept this criterion for distinguishing between belief and knowledge, then it follows that many of our beliefs cannot be considered knowledge. The failure to distinguish between belief and knowledge is a major obstacle to how we as individuals, institutions, and nations interact with one another.

Even though a belief can be false, holding such a belief can still be *rational*.[20] An example of a rational belief would be the belief that it is going to rain tomorrow. You may have formed this belief after listening to the weather report on the radio or seeing a forecast in the newspaper or online. However, since it is possible that it might not rain tomorrow, your belief does not meet the criteria to qualify as knowledge. If you believe that it is raining outside now, you can step outside and confirm it. If it is raining, you have elevated your belief to knowledge; however, all you really know is that it is raining where you are, at the time you step outside. You have no knowledge of where else it may be raining, although you may believe it is raining down the block from where you are.

All knowledge, however, presupposes *truth*. Knowledge has been defined as "justified, *true* belief" (my italics), which recognizes the importance of truth as a condition for knowledge.[21] One theory of truth contends that something is true if, and only if, it corresponds to the facts. Philosopher Bertrand Russell argued that the only thing that can be true or false is a sentence. For example, you make an assertion, and it may be true or false; however, in making the assertion, you are expressing a belief.[22] William Cobern, in his paper "The Nature of Science and the Role of Knowledge and Belief," makes an important observation concerning knowledge and belief: "In everyday language we tend to think of 'knowledge' as reasoned belief that a proposition is true, and the natural sciences provide the archetypal example of what it means to know."[23] However, as I show throughout this book, the prejudices of those who are the gatekeepers of the scientific paradigm seduce us into accepting science as the infallible arbiter of truth and knowledge, and at the same time ignoring the nonmaterial dimensions of reality.

Ira Progroff was a protégé of Carl Jung. He noted that Jung realized that categories of knowledge are "never absolute, although the 'common sense' of every period of history convinces people living within its framework that their particular beliefs about knowledge are fixed and final, universal and eternal."[24] This generational bias can be seen playing out again and again throughout history. Max Planck, the noted theoretical physicist, identified and experienced just such resistance with regard to some new ideas he had on the second law of thermodynamics. Planck, who was instrumental in the discovery of quantum physics, observed firsthand what Jung had identified as a generational bias. In his autobiography, he explained that experiencing such rabid resistance:

> ...gave me also an opportunity to learn a new fact—a remarkable one, in my experience: A new scientific truth does not triumph by convincing its opponents and making them see the light, but rather because its opponents eventually die, and a new generation grows up that is familiar with it.[25]

Another example of Jung's and Planck's generational bias concerns the discoveries of Isaac Newton. His law of gravity was met with stiff resistance. Almost a century after its publication, experiments were still undertaking disproving the law.[26]

The unwillingness to consider both the arguments for and against an idea, or failure to change one's belief if the evidence warrants, is also a long-standing problem for science. There are numerous examples of new discoveries that were met with resistance by noted scientists, as I noted with x-rays.

Yet another example of how scientist's reluctance to even consider "anomalous" cases that are outside the accepted "paradigms" is described by Thomas Kuhn in his book *The Structure of Scientific Revolutions*, in which he referred to "normal science" as that which is based upon past scientific discoveries that the scientific community has acknowledged as worthy of further research. "Extraordinary science" occurs when the profession can no longer evade anomalies that are outside the established paradigm.[27]

It is difficult for some scientists to move their scientific thinking from "normal" to "extraordinary," as evidenced in the view of D. O.

Hebb, a professor of psychology at McGill University. Hebb refused to accept the evidence for telepathy, regardless of how strong the evidence was, because to him, the idea just "did not make sense." He acknowledged that this rejection was simply prejudice.[28]

There is hope, however, that scientists will come to understand the importance of considering information outside the materialist paradigm, and instead of denying such information, will seek to understand and measure its influence. Carl Sagan came to realize there is more to reality than the hard-nosed materialist worldview he had espoused for years. Sagan had made the following statement in his book *Dragons of Eden*: "[The brain's] workings—what we sometimes call mind—are a consequence of its anatomy and physiology and nothing more."[29] However, after reviewing work done by a fellow Cornell professor, Daryl Bem, he stated:

> There are three claims in the ESP field which, in my opinion, deserve serious study: (1) that by thought alone humans can (barely) affect random number generators in computers; (2) that people under mild sensory deprivation can receive thoughts or images projected at them; and (3) that young children sometimes report the details of a previous life, which upon checking turn out to be accurate and which they could not have known about in any other way than reincarnation.[30]

The materialist, scientific approach to a problem can, and often does, fail us. We look to science as the means by which we can convert belief to knowledge, but scientists can also suffer from the inability to consider that which falls outside the particular paradigm within which they are comfortable. Juan Miguel Campanario's paper in the *International Journal of Science Education* illustrates the problem original thinkers had with publishing papers. In his essay, Campanario identifies: 1) scientists who endured unusual difficulties from journal editors and referees when trying to publish papers that eventually became very influential or highly cited in their respective disciplines, 2) some scientists who won the Nobel Prize but whose papers reporting their award-winning discoveries were originally rejected by the editors of scientific journals, and 3) scientists whose discoveries were hindered by the phenomenon of delayed recognition. Some of the scientists whose discoveries are readily identifiable by the public and who were affected by this "resistance to new ideas" include T. Maiman, who wrote a paper on the first laser. His paper was rejected because it did not contain "any significant contribution to basic physics." M. Gell-Mann's paper on quarks was originally rejected for publication; Gell-Mann was subsequently awarded the Nobel Prize for the ideas he presented in that paper. D. I. Armon's paper on plant physiology was hindered by delayed recognition, but it has subsequently become one of the top one hundred most-cited papers in the history of science.[31]

It is understandable why some scientists are excessively wary when presented with research papers that challenge the status quo. However, there are numerous examples of scientists hesitant to disclose their own research because their discoveries are so outside the accepted paradigm that they worry about losing the respect of their peers.

One such case involves Louis Pasteur. The mainstream scientific paradigm of today holds that living organisms arise only from living things and are never created spontaneously. Pasteur conducted an experiment that was designed to prove this principle. In his experiment,

Pasteur prepared several sterile flasks with nutrients and left some open and some sealed. He reported that molds were discovered in the open flasks but not in the sealed ones. However, recently a biologist was able to obtain access to Pasteur's notebooks. In those notebooks, in Pasteur's own hand, he disclosed that life *was* discovered flourishing in the sealed jars. Pasteur had written

> I did not publish these experiments, for the consequences it was necessary to draw from them were too grave for me not to suspect some hidden cause of error in spite of the care I had taken.[32]

There is another reason why it is advisable to defer forming a belief until it is necessary to do so, and that reason has to do with what Marie-Louise von Franz, Carl Jung's protégé, calls "instinctive truth." Instinctive truth is when you "feel something" is not quite truthful, but you do not have a rational reason for your suspicions. Instinctive truth is not "intuition," which can be either right or wrong. According to von Franz, instinctive truth is a manifestation of the Self and has nothing to do with intuition. She describes the difference between intuition and instinct:

> Intuition can be 50% right and 50% wrong...It is better not to trust intuition all the time, for it may be blurred by projection...But the instinctive truth... is something which operates in every human being, a discreetly quick word which the Self whispers in your ear and which generally you are too slow to catch or you, yourself, talk too much and "it" cannot be heard.[33]

If one had already formed a belief about someone or something, they might not recognize the warning signs that instinctive truth is attempting to communicate. This might be the case where you want something so badly that you lower the threshold for critical discernment. If you form a belief that someone is "a good person who would never lie or take advantage of you" and then are told something by this person, you might not acknowledge any doubts arising in your mind, as this would be in conflict with your belief in the honesty of the individual—you wouldn't be able to "hear" the Self warning you.

Like skepticism, a bias in one's view of something can adversely affect the ability to make a good decision; they are unlikely to act in a way that will create the uncomfortable dissonance discussed above. Festinger observed:

> One would expect such a person to have very positive and one-sided opinions about many issues and not be able, very effectively, to see "both sides of a question." If this is correct, one would then find the almost paradoxical situation where a person who is very "decided" concerning opinions, issues and values also shows an inability to make decisions.[34]

Belief does spur us to action, and some actions spurred by false beliefs can have unfortunate consequences. Bertrand Russell argued that belief *promotes* behavior: "A belief is a state of an organism promoting behavior such as a certain occurrence would promote if sensibly present; the occurrence which would promote this behavior is the 'significance' of the belief."[35]

Still another reason to not adhere strongly to beliefs until it is necessary to take action has to do with creativity. In an article titled "What Happens to Creativity as We Age?" the author asks,

> Why does creativity generally tend to decline as we age? One reason may be that as we grow older, we know more. That is mostly an advantage, of course. But it also may lead us to ignore evidence that contradicts what we already think. We become too set in our ways to change.[36]

If we want to increase our creativity, we should examine the beliefs we hold strongly and try to formulate an argument in support of the other side of that belief. In so doing, we should look at all the research and information available to understand the other side of that belief. If our beliefs are not shaken, we will at least come to better understand why some individuals believe as they do. Furthermore, by practicing this exercise frequently, one will become more tolerant of others who do not see the world as they do; they may also find themselves becoming more receptive to new ideas, resulting in greater creativity.[37] The important thing about beliefs is knowing that they are, in fact, beliefs and not knowledge.[38] For example, you may believe that plants and animals have some elements of consciousness (and there is much evidence to support you, as I show in a later chapter), but you should be receptive to information that will both challenge your belief as well as reinforce it, and you should respect the beliefs of others that may be in conflict with yours. If having a belief brings you peace and joy, then so be it!

There are times when beliefs can be beneficial—even lifesaving. Prayer is one such manifestation of belief that has been shown to be effective and is perhaps one of the most notable examples of a so-called irrational belief. For that reason, looking at the effect prayer can have on the sick and disabled can be instructive. Rupert Sheldrake relates the following about prayer:

> In several independent series of experiments, some people were prayed for while others were not. These experiments were conducted according to standard double-blind procedures, as in clinical trials. The patients themselves did not know they were being prayed for, nor did their physicians. Nevertheless, those who were prayed for without their knowing it tended to survive better or heal more quickly than those who were not prayed for. Of those who pray... most would probably agree that the focusing of their intention provides a channel for healing grace or divine power.[39]

Even the popular press has recognized that there might be something to the idea of prayer. Radin relates a 1996 cover story that asked, "Can prayer, faith and spirituality really improve your physical health? A growing and surprising body of scientific evidence say they can."[40]

Yet another example of the power of belief is the placebo effect. Author Michael Talbot recounts a case in which some doctors conducted an experiment on patients who complained of recurrent pain in the chest and left arm due to reduced blood flow to the heart. Instead of performing the usual surgical procedure, they cut open the patients and then merely sewed them back up again. The patients who received the fake surgical solution reported the same relief as those patients who received the actual surgery. In effect, the patients who "believed" they were receiving the pain-relieving surgery were merely experiencing a placebo effect.[41] In a further example of the effectiveness of belief, Talbot notes that injection of caffeine into caffeine-sensitive individuals won't keep them awake if they believe they've been given a sedative.[42] Talbot adds,

> In addition to angina pectoris, conditions that have proved responsive to placebo treatment include migraine headaches, allergies, fever, the common cold, acne, asthma, warts, various kinds of pain, nausea and seasickness, peptic ulcers, psychiatric syndromes such as depression and anxiety, rheumatoid and degenerative arthritis, diabetes, radiation sickness, Parkinsonism, multiple sclerosis, and cancer.[43]

What should be clear from reading this chapter is that belief can be a double-edged sword. It can be the cause of conflict between people, institutions, and countries. The lack of tolerance for the beliefs of others is a principal cause of the disharmony we see both domestically and internationally in both religion and politics. However, belief can also be used for good. Believing in the sanctity of all life and in tolerance for the beliefs of others is a first step toward achieving peace on earth.

2

The Evidence for an Ultimate Reality

What matters, what's at the heart of the subject, is whether there exist realms that challenge convention by suggesting that what we've long thought to be the universe is only one component of a far grander, perhaps far stranger, and mostly hidden reality.

—Brian Greene

Now, my own suspicion is that the universe is not only queerer than we suppose, but queerer than we can suppose.

—J. B. S. Haldane

It must be understood that the world into which these [visionaries] probed is perfectly real. Its reality is more irrefutable and more coherent than that of the empirical world, where reality is perceived by the senses…This world is hidden behind the very act of

sense perception and has to be sought underneath
its apparent objective certainty.
—Henry Corbin

It is the soul which, by the divine creative power
inherent in it, makes the metaphysical assertion; it
posits the distinctions between metaphysical entities. Not only is it the condition of all metaphysical
reality, it is that reality.
—Carl Jung

If the doors of perception were cleansed everything
would appear to man as it is, infinite.
—William Blake

THE HIDDEN REALITY, A NONPERCEPTUAL aspect of the one reality, manifests in our perceptual world. The evidence of extradimensional sources of influence on the material world is found in such diverse fields as psychology, physics, biology. It is also found by individuals who have experienced this superordinate realm in altered states of consciousness.

Nature of the Hidden Realm
This hidden realm is that which Huxley refers to in his book *The Doors of Perception*. It is a realm that, although beyond our perception, manifests in the visible world. This hidden reality is such that, for those who are fortunate enough to pass into it through the doors of perception "will never be the same…[they] will be wiser…happier…better equipped to understand…the unfathomable Mystery."[44]

"Hidden reality," "ultimate reality," and "divine realm" are terms used interchangeably throughout this book. It is a realm whose existence can be inferred from its influence on

- the psyche through the operation of archetypal constituents, including experiences of the numinous;

- the micro world through its effects on quantum wave/particle duality which exhibit properties such as quantum entanglement and complementarity and which are not explainable in Newtonian scientific terms; and

- inanimate matter through the ubiquity of consciousness and morphogenetic fields.

Evidence in Psychology

Ken Wilbur, a transpersonal psychologist, has discovered the benefits of including other disciplines in his practice.[45] He has extended his studies into the areas of philosophy, mysticism, and quantum physics. He considers transpersonal psychology as "a sustained and experimental inquiry into spiritual, transcendental, or perennial philosophical concerns."[46] Perennial philosophical concerns include exploring the nature of ultimate reality.

Stanislav Grof, a Czech psychiatrist, recognizes the failure of Western science to consider phenomena that cannot be objectively measured and observed, noting that "perennial philosophy acknowledges an entire hierarchy of realities—some of them manifest, others hidden under ordinary circumstances and directly observable only in certain special states of consciousness."[47] The "perennial philosophy," or *philosophia perennis*, alluded to by both Wilbur and Grof had its genesis in the writings of Gottfried Wilhelm Leibniz, a brilliant German philosopher. It is a philosophy that holds that all religious traditions share a single metaphysical truth. Leibniz believed, along with Plato, Descartes, and Spinoza, that human reason was capable of discovering this truth.

Carl Jung wrote his biography *Memories, Dreams, Reflections* when he was eighty-one years old. In it, he recounts his dream discovery of "a collective a priori beneath the personal psyche."[48] The a priori to which he refers is the collective unconscious of the psyche that extends beyond the realm of the personal. This collective unconscious, or transpersonal level of the psyche, is seamlessly connected to the individual's psyche and may be thought of metaphorically as the mind of God.[49] The collective unconscious is an attribute of ultimate reality.

"Collective unconscious" and "transpersonal Self" are terms often used interchangeably. They reflect the view that there is a "unified field of consciousness that affects inner and outer at the same time." Lionel Corbett, an MD who teaches depth psychology, argues that the spiritual dimension of the psyche is vast—it may "permeate the entire world of nature, and even the entire cosmos."[50] Mathematician Karl Gustav Jacobi agrees on the enormity of this dimension, considering the collective unconscious as a "suprapersonal matrix... an inner cosmos as infinite as the cosmos outside us."[51] Although consciousness and matter are seen as dissimilar, some have argued that they both arose out of a common order, in which the workings of matter and the activity of information are just two sides of the one reality, both hidden and visible.[52]

Jung considers the collective unconscious as a collection of "mythological motifs or primordial images...the whole of mythology could be taken as a sort of projection of the collective unconscious."[53] Von Franz considers the unconscious as playing a miraculous role by delivering models that can be arrived at directly from within without looking at outer facts, and that afterward seem to fit outer reality. Is that a miracle or not? There are two possible explanations: either the unconscious knows about other realities, or what we call the unconscious is a part of the same thing as outer reality, for we do not know how the unconscious is linked with matter.[54]

Von Franz brings up the question as to whether our unconscious is aware of other realities. If this is true, it might help us understand what is happening when we experience those other realities in an altered state of consciousness.

An archetype is a universal pattern of human nature. The archetype that arises from this "supra-personal matrix," is considered to be a transpersonal self-organizing principle within consciousness whose origin is unknown,[55] and which manifests as images, or symbols in dreams, mythology, synchronicities, and projections.[56] These archetypes are important to psychology in understanding behavior, and they manifest a spiritual principle within the psyche. This spiritual principle is ubiquitous and cannot be considered the unique province of any single religious doctrine.[57] All religious traditions incorporate some form of ritualistic behavior, suggesting that this behavior is archetypally influenced.

Jung supported this notion of a spiritual principle within the psyche. He considered the universal belief in spirits to be a direct expression of the archetypal influence of the unconscious.[58] He noted that the collective unconscious can be experienced but not controlled. He felt that the collective unconscious "is either the *medium* for the transmission of numinous experiences from a transcendent divinity beyond the psyche, or the numinous experience may be a direct experience with the autonomous (objective) psyche itself."[59]

Our understanding of the collective unconscious is that it is a vast, nonmaterial realm. As Jeremy Taylor says, "The reality of this realm is demonstrated by the spontaneous appearance of archetypal forms."[60] This realm acts upon and influences the personal psyche. One way in which it does this is through the symbolism presented in dreams. This spontaneous appearance of archetypal forms is a manifestation of the nonphysical, hidden reality acting upon objective reality through operation of the psyche.

In a paper presented in *Behavioral Sciences*, Ponte, Valadas, and Schäfer make the following observation concerning the relationship of Jung's archetypes to quantum physics:

> If we want to characterize Carl Jung's psychology in one sentence, we can say that Analytical Psychology, embodied in the archetype structure, leads us to the view that there is a part of the world that we can't see, a realm of reality that doesn't consist of material things but of non-material forms. These forms are real even though they are invisible because they have the potential to appear in our mind and act in it.[61]

One way this transpersonal realm influences the material world is through its effects on the psyche; there are, however, other ways in which its effects are manifested in the material world, as the discussion continues.

Evidence in Physics

Paul Davies, a physicist at Arizona State University, is one of a growing number of scientists open to the idea of a hidden or divine realm. In his book *The Mind of God*, he notes,

Sooner or later we all have to accept something as given, whether it is God, or logic, or a set of laws, or some other foundation for existence. Thus, "ultimate" questions will always lie beyond the scope of empirical science as it is usually defined…Among those scientists who are not religious in a conventional sense, many confess to a vague feeling that there is "something" beyond the surface of daily experience, some meaning behind experience… Through my scientific work I have come to believe that the universe is put together with an ingenuity so astonishing that I cannot merely accept it as a brute fact.[62]

David Bohm was a professor of theoretical physics at Birkbeck College who made significant contributions to the field of quantum physics. His theories involved a new assumption about the nature of matter. He theorized that quantum particles are represented by fluctuations within a quantum field, and that those particles exhibit a quantum potential: "The quantum potential is…subtle in its form and does not fall off with distance…even objects which are at remote distances from the quantum particle can still have a profound effect on it."[63] This quantum potential has something in common with the mechanism by which Sheldrake's morphic field acts on an organism (see "Evidence in Biology"). Bohm is describing a place in which "it is possible to look at the universe we know and all that lies within it and perceive it in a new way."[64] David Bohm has argued that "particles have to be taken literally as projections of a higher-dimensional reality [an ultimate reality] which cannot be accounted for in terms of any force of interaction between them."[65] The quantum particles to which

Bohm refers exhibit very strange attributes, which are observed in "wave-particle duality" and "quantum entanglement."

Wave-particle duality refers to the fact that subatomic units of matter cannot be labeled as waves or particles because they have a dual nature. Sometimes they behave as waves, and at other times they manifest as particles, depending on our observation of them and how we have set up to measure them. Before a measurement is taken, they are neither particles nor waves, but rather exhibit the potential to be either, depending on the measurement apparatus.[66]

Quantum entanglement occurs when our observation of a quantum object causes it to manifest, simultaneously influencing its correlated twin object, irrespective of the distance between the two objects.[67] Although the fact of quantum entanglement was proven and accepted by mainstream science, Einstein continued to be uncomfortable with the idea, calling it "spooky action at a distance."[68]

Bohm, on the other hand, recognized this universal connectedness of things and events, which he considered a basic aspect of quantum reality.[69] His causal interpretation of the quantum potential "suggests that matter has orders that are closer to that of a mind than to a simple mechanical order."[70] He believed that there was a deeper reality than that which was detectable through our senses. He called this the "implicate order"—an "undivided holistic realm that is beyond concepts like space-time, matter, or energy."[71] "Implicate order" comes from the verb "to implicate," which means to fold inward. In support of his theory, Bohm offered two examples of how this order manifests in the world of everyday reality.

The first example involves placing a drop of ink in a liquid such as glycerin. The glycerin is then stirred very slowly in one direction until the drop of ink completely disappears in the glycerin. If the glycerin is then stirred in the opposite direction, the drop of ink reappears.

This experiment, Bohm argues, illustrates an expression of a high degree of *hidden* order.[72] In other words, even when the order is no longer visible, it continues to exist.

The second example concerns the way in which a television receiver functions. The picture appearing on the television screen has first been viewed through a camera and then transformed into an electrical signal. That signal is then carried by radio waves, which are picked up by an antenna (this was before cable!) and transformed back into an electrical signal, which then appears on the television screen. This example is meant to illustrate the process of a transformation from visible images to subtler forms of energy and back again to manifest as visible images once again.

Bernard d'Espagnat of the University of Paris acknowledges, in agreement with Bohm, that there is a universal connectedness. He concluded that "[t]he violation of separability seems to imply that in some sense all these objects constitute an indivisible whole."[73] Jane Carr notes in her thesis that "Everything that one sees, hears, tastes, touches, feels, everything in the hear-and-now [*sic*], including consciousness, is forever connected."[74]

The applicability of quantum entanglement to the macroworld has been an important topic of debate among scientists since its discovery. The reality of nonlocality requires accepting that we live in an instantaneously connected world in which everything is connected and cannot be separated.[75] Bell's proof of nonlocal ultimate reality is thus the contemporary echo from mathematics of the ancient mystic's claim: "We are all one."

Bohm further explains the heightened role that consciousness plays in determining reality at all levels. He and others have argued that physical objects and spiritual values share a similar reality. This view was shared by theoretical physicist Eugene Wigner, who stated "this [connectedness of life and matter] is the only known position that can be consistent with quantum mechanics."[76] Bohm clarified his thoughts in a dialogue with philosopher Renée Weber. The relevant parts of this exchange are reproduced here:

> **WEBER.** Mathematics is pure thought.

> **BOHM.** That's right. You won't find it anywhere in matter.

> **WEBER.** You are saying that even today's physicists, who might be least inclined toward anything spiritual, are practically forced to assume that it is beyond the material.

> **BOHM.** Physicists may not accept this, but they are attributing qualities to matter that are beyond those usually considered to be material…the mystic sees in matter an immanent principle of unity, and this is implicitly what the scientists are also doing…matter was found to be far more subtle than we supposed, both for quantum mechanics and relativity.

> **WEBER.** Does "subtle" imply spiritual?

> **BOHM.** It moves in that direction.[77]

I interpret this exchange as confirmation of Bohm's recognition of the spiritual dimension of matter. Although as a physicist, he is guarded in his assertions, it is clear that Bohm considered the distinction between matter and spirit to be far less robust than what was assumed under the Newtonian physics paradigm.

Bohm looked for a model that would illustrate his notion of "undivided wholeness" and concluded that a hologram incorporated features that were consistent with his model. Each small snippet of a holographic image contains the entire image, in contrast to a traditional photograph. He saw the hologram as analogous to the storage area of memory in the brain. Others, including mathematical physicist Roger Penrose, have argued that memory may not be stored in the brain at all, but may be stored in cells throughout the body or in a "field."[78] Bohm made reference to such a field when he stated, "This is very similar to what Sheldrake calls a 'morphogenetic field or morphic resonance'...such a field would not be located anywhere [in time or space]."[79]

Evidence in Biology

Rupert Sheldrake holds a PhD in biochemistry from the University of Cambridge. He is a biologist and author of more than eighty-five scientific papers and nine books, and is the coauthor of six books. His theories, however unfashionable, unconventional, or unorthodox, deserve at least to be seriously considered by scientists with an open mind. Mainstream science has subjected his theory of morphogenetic fields, mentioned above in the quote from Bohm, to harsh criticism, failing to even consider it worthy of testing and experimentation. As an example his book *A New Science of Life* was attacked by the senior editor of the prestigious publication *Nature* as "pseudo-science" and "worthy of burning."[80] Attacks of this kind are evidence of the resistance to changes in the scientific paradigm studied by Thomas Kuhn and mentioned in Chapter 1. Fortunately, some scientists have seriously considered the merits of Sheldrake's theories. Stanislav Grof, mentioned earlier, was one of the founders of transpersonal psychology; he offers a different view of Sheldrake's work:

> Sheldrake has offered a brilliant critique of the limitations of the explanatory power of mechanistic science and its inability to face problems of basic significance in the areas of morphogenesis during individual development and evolution of species, genetics, instinctual and more complex forms of behavior.[81]

Sheldrake argues that morphogenetic fields are fields of information that influence the structure and form of both animate and inanimate matter. They embody a kind of knowing, a knowing of *how* to grow and *what* to grow into.[82] This idea of fields of knowing is consistent with the new scientific paradigms that have emerged from quantum physics. Two of these new paradigms are:

- That at a deep level, there is a dimension of information that creates form out of formlessness by influencing the behavior of matter, placing it in a formation that will exhibit properties of matter.

- Empty space is not "nothingness," but rather a fullness and reservoir of nonmaterial intelligence.[83]

The influence of this field can be seen in the turning in unison of a flock of birds or a school of fish. The field informs, directs, and holds the individual units of the group together. Sheldrake further maintains that we receive the effects of the past behaviors of our own species, which strikes a parallel with Jung's idea of a collective unconscious and Bohm's idea of the implicate order. These morphogenetic fields connect similar things across space without any known way in which they could be connected (in the Newtonian paradigm sense), and, he argues, they connect things together across time. These fields, similar to electromagnetic fields and comparable to Bohm's television receiver metaphor, are what dictate the shapes of plants and animals. The species is modified by the environment, and in turn, the modified plants and animals exert an influence on the morphogenetic field.[84] This idea of a "feedback loop" is comparable to what Jung says about archetypes.

In another work by Sheldrake, *The Sense of Being Stared At*, he introduces in some detail his theory on extended minds. He suggests that minds are not confined to heads but stretch out beyond them.[85] He skirts the issue of mind-over-matter effects but argues that there is much evidence that people can influence physical events at a distance through their intentions.

A major stumbling block to Sheldrake's ideas seems to be the absence of an acceptable explanation or theory about how it all works. Sheldrake argues in reply that there is evidence from reliable, well-controlled experiments that shows that people can influence physical events through their intentions, and that his theory of extended minds is consistent with the results of those experiments.[86]

Thomas Kuhn was a pioneer in recognizing resistance to new ideas. He describes the problem that discoveries made outside the traditional accepted paradigms face in his book *The Structure of Scientific Revolutions*. Kuhn's observations are particularly relevant to the works of Sheldrake because of the staunch resistance and dismissal of his ideas without serious investigation. Even before Kuhn's landmark work, Heisenberg, a founder of quantum mechanics, had this to say about scientists in general, which also applies to the dismissal of Sheldrake's works:

> From what has been said, one would be inclined to demand that the scientist should never rely on special doctrines, never confine his method of thinking to a special philosophy. He should always be prepared to have the foundations of his knowledge changed by new experience.[87]

The Need for a Paradigm Change

Sheldrake notes that the Cartesian mechanistic paradigm is still the rule rather than the exception today, particularly in biology and medicine. It is also interesting that this materialistic world view arose from ancient "mystical" religions, which saw reality as timeless and changeless. A definition of mysticism that is apropos to this discussion is "[b]elief that direct knowledge of God, spiritual truth, or Ultimate Reality can be attained through subjective experience."[88] Although mysticism is slowly gaining respectability in the age of quantum mechanics, we don't fully understand what mysticism is or what mystical experience is telling us. However, we don't fully understand quantum mechanics either.[89]

"Mysticism" is a word that many scientists consider pejoratively. This aversion to the idea that mysticism can help us understand ultimate reality arises principally from two sources. First, there is a failure on the part of some scientists to venture outside a materialist scientific paradigm, a paradigm that formed the foundation for their education in the sciences. Secondly, in some cases, a scientist's career may suffer if he or she shows tolerance to anything that might be even remotely supportive of the idea that there may be a spiritual, nonphysical aspect of reality, an underlying principle of mysticism.

Wolfgang Pauli, a Nobel Prize–winning physicist stated in 1957, "My real problem was and still is the relation between Mysticism and Science, what is different between them and what is common. Both mystics and science have the same aim, to become aware of the unity of knowledge."[90] Today, the words "mystical" or "mysticism" are eschewed by many scientists who steadfastly cling to the Newtonian mechanistic paradigm.[91]

Those serious scientists who desire to obtain funding for a research project, or have a paper published in prestigious journal, or gain tenure at their university, will often go to great lengths to avoid acknowledging or recognizing anything that might be called "mysticism." But what does that word mean, and why is it so abhorrent to serious scientists? There are many definitions of mysticism and doubtless just as many connotations of the term.

Paul Kurtz, considered by some to be a leading secular humanist philosopher, was also a vocal skeptic on all things outside the materialist paradigm. In his book *The Transcendent Temptation*, he explains his interpretation of a mystical experience:

> Mystics claim that over and beyond these normal forms of awareness there is another range of consciousness in which we come into contact with a reality much deeper, more authentic and enduring than anything we confront in everyday life. They are unable to translate this reality into meaningful perceptual or conceptual equivalents…It is "ineffable," they insist, unutterable and indefinable.[92]

Kurtz's observation is an accurate explanation of how mystics often describe their experience of the hidden reality. His problem with such experiences is "that mysticism, by its very nature, violates the standards of scientific objectivity." He points out that there are differences between Eastern and Western descriptions of mystical experiences, but that they share the common characteristic of "the apprehension of an ultimate 'nonsensuous unity' to all things, a powerful sense of the 'oneness to reality.'"[93] Of course, this is exactly what we are told in descriptions of the subatomic realm: a realm in which all is connected through the phenomenon of entanglement—in other words, the "oneness" of reality!

An investigation into the nature of mysticism and mystical experiences may be helpful in understanding even more about how and why observer participation is necessary for the collapse of the wave function in quantum physics. The collapse of the wave function is the act of converting an immaterial probability into an actual particle.[94] If observer participation is requisite for this quantum event, perhaps macroevents (which, after all, consist of microevents) require participation of an observer. The desire to distinguish this strange but verifiable conversion of a probability into a material object, from anything that might be characterized as "mysticism," is often argued by scientists. Consider the views of two physicists:

> Since quantum mechanics can make Nature appear almost *mystical*, some people become susceptible to wholly unjustified notions. They can be misled onto accepting supernatural foolishness...Sometimes we physicists hesitate to call attention to this strangeness [of quantum mechanics] because *it can make physics seem mystical* (italics mine).[95]

Surely it is not a great leap to suggest that the strangeness to which these two physicists refer could justifiably come under the "mystical" rubric. Somewhat surprising is the fact that even today, the resistance to a paradigm change that recognizes the proven importance of consciousness in quantum events is unjustifiably resolute. This same resistance to recognizing how something nonphysical (consciousness) can influence the material world impedes the ability to find funding for research programs in other fields such as extrasensory perception and psychokinesis. A debate between Caltech physicist Sean Carroll and a Buddhist scholar is illustrative.

In the debate, Carroll argues in reference to the possibility of true psychic powers that "we know that there aren't new particles or forces out there yet to be discovered that would support them. Not simply because we have not found them yet, but because we definitely would have found them if they had the right characteristics to give us the requisite powers."[96] In a recent paper, Lawrence Bonchek, MD, stated that people "too often assume if proof is hypothetically obtainable but lacking, the proposition must be false. It is this error that makes it so important to emphasize that absence of evidence is not evidence of absence."[97] Bonchek uses this argument to defend weaknesses in the Darwinian theory of evolution. It is relevant here to show the error in Carroll's statement that "we know that there aren't new particles or forces out there yet to be discovered." Somehow Carroll didn't get the message that absence of evidence is not evidence of absence. Sometimes the evidence shows up later, as in this recent statement from CERN Labs: "Fresh evidence of an unknown particle that could carry a fifth force of nature gives the NA64 collaboration at CERN a new incentive to continue searches." Why should they continue to search when Carroll assures us there are no new particles to discover?

Later in the debate, Carroll assures us that he knows that there is no "life after death." Carroll is an erudite, eloquent speaker whose confidence and demeanor can mislead those who fail to look more deeply at what is being said. Carroll's conceit must serve as a caution to all who search for the truth; even highly educated individuals are capable of arguing from ignorance.

In this chapter, I have advanced the idea that it is important to explore the manifestations of this hidden, ultimate reality in order to fully understand that there is something missing in the dogma of materialist science. Corbett observes that many today have given up on traditional religion because it fails them in times of crisis.[98] Recognizing and accepting the idea of a superordinate realm, a realm with real, tangible, testable evidence found in our day-to-day reality, may bring comfort to those for whom religion has failed.

3

Synchronicity

The general category of law, which includes the causal laws, the laws of chance, and the laws relating these two classes of law, we shall call by the name of laws of nature.
—David Bohm[99]

[T]hese experiments prove that the psyche at times functions outside of the spatio-temporal law of causality. This indicates that our conceptions of space and time, and therefore of causality also, are incomplete.
—Carl Jung[100]

The new reality [quantum physics] has dissolved causality because the theory of relativity revealed that the fixed arrow of time is an illusion, a misapprehension sustained by the classical assumptions of an absolute space and time.
—Dean Radin[101]

> Coincidence is God's way of remaining anonymous.
> —Albert Einstein

> Just as causality describes the sequence of events, so synchronicity to the Chinese mind deals with the coincidence of events. The causal point of view tells us a dramatic story about how D came into existence: it took its origin from C, which existed before D, and C in its turn had a father, B, etc. The synchronistic view on the other hand tries to produce an equally meaningful picture of coincidence.
> —Richard Wilhelm[102]

Causality

This chapter investigates the relationship between two (or more) events and the difficulties in attempting to assign the terms *causality*, *coincidence*, *seriality*, *serendipity*, or *synchronicity* to those relationships. Although most individuals have an idea of what "causality" is, defining it precisely becomes problematic. Clearly it is not sufficient to say that A caused B because A preceded B (the post hoc, ergo propter hoc fallacy: *after this, therefore because of this*). In law, for example, an individual ought to have been reasonably able to foresee the effects of his actions (or lack of actions) in order to be held liable for damage; the moral aspect of this test is that "ought" implies "can." However, not every instance in which the doctrine of "ought" implying "can" is definitive: the application of some other law may provide an exception.

Consider the example of Abraham Lincoln's death. In searching for a cause, how far back does one go? Was it the bullet in the gun? Was it the manufacturer of the gun? Talbot adds up all of the events which led to the invention of the gun, all the reasons Booth wanted to kill Lincoln, even "the evolution of the human race that allowed for the development of the gun."[103] How far back from an effect do you go in finding the cause?

We often think about causality as the last event A before event B, after which there was no reasonable action that could have changed the occurrence of the event. However, Russell, in an early paper (1912), argued that no matter how short the time interval was between cause and effect, "something may happen during this interval which prevents the expected result." If the possible interference of the environment is considered, the "probability of repetition is diminished, until at last, when the whole environment is included, the probability becomes almost *nil*."[104] This philosophical argument seems to deny causality altogether.

Nuclear physicist David Bohm recognized that an effect could have an infinite number of causes, but most of them have a negligible effect on the problem. This conclusion follows from quantum theory that all events and objects in the universe are connected. He argued that "[i]n real problems, it is very rarely possible to deal with *all* the causes that are significant."[105]

Trying to understand causality leads to the more important question: Does causality, as the term is commonly used, actually exist? In our everyday world, we take it for granted that almost always when an event occurs, something caused it. This is the Western way of thinking, which is very different from that of Eastern philosophy. Jung noted that any event being observed is more of a chance hit according to the ancient Chinese view rather than a causally connected chain of events leading up to it, as in Western thought.[106] He makes the following statement in his foreword to *The I Ching or Book of Changes*:

> Our science…is based upon the principle of causality, and causality is considered to be an axiomatic truth. What Kant's Critique of Pure Reason failed to do, is being accomplished by modern physics. The axioms of causality are being shaken to their foundations: we know now that what we term natural laws are merely statistical truths and thus must necessarily allow for exceptions.[107]

Jung further distinguished Western concepts of causality from that of Eastern concepts by noting that "Chinese science is based upon the principle of synchronicity, or parallelism in time, which is naturally regarded by us as superstition." Jung's comment was in reference to physicist Pascual Jordan's idea that telepathy between a sender and a receiver involved the sensing of the same object simultaneously in a common conscious space: "Jung was ecstatic that a physicist of such high repute was interested in the paranormal."[108]

To Jung, the connection of two events through the mechanism of causality required a "transmission of energy from the cause to the effect."[109] By exploring the way in which events are connected and considering not only causality but also coincidence, seriality, serendipity, and synchronicity, we may discover that the way in which nature connects things and events is through a "hidden structure" of order.

At the quantum (subatomic) level, the interconnectedness of events is one of the most important discoveries in quantum physics. As I have shown, quantum theory has established the reality of universal interconnectedness of all things. The world cannot be broken down into independently existing parts.[110] At the sub-micro-quantum level, this "interconnectedness" is called "entanglement." Entanglement refers to the behavior of all things and events at the quantum level; it is not dependent on any of the several mathematical theories explaining quantum theory. Bohm acknowledges this interconnectedness where he states, "[W]e say that inseparable quantum interconnectedness of the whole universe is the fundamental reality, and that relatively independently behaving parts are merely particular and contingent forms within this whole."[111]

This interconnectedness also applies to the psychological makeup of the individual. Jung pointed out that the collective unconscious is a ubiquitous continuum, present everywhere; thus, when an event occurs that comes into contact with this collective unconscious, its influence is everywhere.[112]

Einstein was deeply troubled by the fact that at the quantum level, there are no causes at separate alternative events. Dr. Johnjoe McFadden, a professor of molecular genetics, notes that at the quantum level there is no way of knowing which slit a photon will travel through. It is entirely random—there is no cause separating alternative events.[113] In truth, we only dimly understand the way in which those noncausal connections operate.[114]

It is somewhat of a conundrum that we are attempting to unpack the meanings of terms used to describe how two or more events may be connected in the macroworld, when at the very smallest scale, all events are described as "interconnected" and "acausal." Perhaps the real questions should be: Is "causality" a meaningful term at all? Are events interconnected with other events in different ways? This difficulty was recognized by Jung, who acknowledged that while we might look for acausal events in the macroworld, we would not recognize them "for the simple reason that we cannot imagine events that are connected non-causally and are capable of a non-causal explanation."[115]

Coincidence

With respect to coincidence, Dr. Bernard Beitman notes there are two important variables in looking at two (or more) events to determine if they are a coincidence: the time interval between the events and the degree to which they exhibit similarity. He also mentions secondary characteristics of surprise and ownership. Understanding the nature of connections of two or more events that may be considered a "coincidence" is important to many topics discussed in this book, such as paranormal phenomena.[116]

According to Beitman, coincidence is something that individuals perceive by recognizing patterns in the environment that correspond with their own mental and emotional gestalt. This perception of "coincidence" emerges from swirls of information in our minds that match events in our surroundings. Like two dials spun by separate hands, mind and environment briefly coincide and produce an unlikely correspondence. The correspondence strikes us because it is unusual, often surprising, and sometimes wildly improbable.[117]

Once it has been established that two or more events constitute a coincidence, it is important to determine under which of the three different classifications of the events fall: seriality, serendipity, or synchronicity.

Two mathematicians, Diaconis and Mosteller, wrote a paper discussing methods that could be used to study the various kinds of coincidences. They concluded, in agreement with Kammerer and Jung, that we are "swimming in an ocean of coincidences." They consider that nature and we ourselves are "creating these [coincidences], sometimes causally, and also partly through the perception and partly through objective accidental relationships."[118]

The German philosopher Arthur Schopenhauer concluded that coincidence represented the simultaneous occurrence of events that were not causally connected. He further suggested that all the events that occur in life are connected in two different ways: "firstly, in the objective, causal connection of the natural process; secondly, in a subjective connection which exists only in relation to the individual who experiences it."[119]

Seriality

Seriality has been defined as "a series of events in the objective world that the mind takes note of and remembers." Such a series does not necessarily include subjective elements; the observations are verifiable through objective means.[120]

Paul Kammerer was an Austrian biologist who is best known for having advocated the controversial Lamarckian theory of the inheritance of acquired characteristics.[121] Lesser known is his work *The Law of Series*, which he published in 1919. In that study, Kammerer noted the repetition of similar events over a fifteen-year period, concluding, "We thus arrive at the image of a world-mosaic or cosmic kaleidoscope, which, in spite of constant shufflings and rearrangements, also takes care of bringing like and like together."[122] He studied seriality in depth, defining it as a recurrence of the same or similar things and events clustering in time or space. These recurrences are not "connected by the same active cause,"[123] but instead are the products of hidden structure manifesting in an evolution from the "barely coincidental to the powerfully unusual,"[124] such as that alluded to by Mansfield, and to which I referred in Chapter 2.

Kammerer contended that coincidences are the "peaks" of a larger ocean of organized information below the surface of perceptual reality. His theory of seriality shares much with the theories of chaos, complexity, and catastrophe.[125] Jung studiously considered Kammerer's theory of seriality in developing his own theory of synchronicity. Jung viewed synchronicity as differing from seriality in that the connections between events were seen as due to meaning, rather than an occasional manifestation of organized information outside of objective reality.[126]

Serendipity

"Serendipity" is a word describing a certain kind of coincidence. The word originated with Horace Walpole, who conceived of it after reading a fairy tale in which the word "Serendip" was used. He used it to describe his discovery of something that he did not expect. It has been described as "one of the ten English words hardest to translate."[127] There are some examples of discoveries that have been considered "serendipitous," which can be found in Wikipedia. One writer defines "serendipity" as a phenomenon that occurs "when events result in unexpected discoveries which are considered fortunate or useful."[128] Walpole considered serendipity "to mean finding something both by formed observation...and by accident."[129] In science, we get a more helpful definition: "finding something when looking for something else."[130] Today the term has come to include finding something by luck or chance as well. Serendipity does not imply a connection through meaning, which distinguishes it from synchronicity.[131]

Synchronicity

Synchronicity is a term conceived by Jung as:

> [A] seemingly significant coincidence in time of two
> or more events that are related but not causally con-
> nected, as when a dream turns out to correspond to
> an external event or when close relatives or friends

have similar thoughts, dreams, or experiences at
the same time.[132]

Synchronicity is an important concept to understand because it
is illustrative of a way in which two unrelated events are connected,
in sharp contrast to cause and effect. It important in both philosophy
and psychology; it is also important because it may help to understand
the operation of parapsychological phenomena such as extrasensory
perception (ESP). ESP is the reception of information through the
mind, as opposed to the recognized physical senses.

Jung considered his theory of synchronicity to be much more
scientific, even claiming, in contrast to Kammerer's claim of acausality for seriality, that the examples offered by Kammerer were "reducible, if not to a common cause, then at least to several causes,"
and were therefore not acausal.[133] Jung was critical of Kammerer's
seriality, claiming "[h]is concepts of seriality, imitation, attraction,
and inertia belong to a causally conceived view of the world and tell
us no more than that the run of chance corresponds to statistical and
mathematical probability."

I take exception to Jung's claim that causes can be found in
Kammerer's examples of seriality; I suspect that Jung was merely
trying to distinguish seriality from the theory of synchronicity which
he was proposing. It seems reasonable to me that there is an overlap
in coincidences that can be considered as examples of seriality and
those that can be considered synchronistic. Surely there are gradations
of meaning. The meaning of events connected through seriality may
be of a different magnitude than those connected through Jung's
synchronicity; they may have meaning by virtue of their statistically
improbable occurrence, as my experience at the end of this chapter
will show.

Jung believed that his theory of a connection between events through meaning was a complementary theory to that of causality. With the help of physicist Wolfgang Pauli, he was able to argue that the complementary aspect of waves and particles at the quantum level, which is necessary to understand quantum phenomena, is analogous to causality and synchronicity. Both causality and synchronicity, to Jung, are necessary to understand the relationship more fully between events in the material world.[134]

Synchronicity is evidence of the interconnectedness of things material and immaterial, such as when a nonmaterial dream is closely followed by an objective event.[135] Synchronicity is evidence of a "cosmos in which seemingly unrelated events are woven together to form a continuous world fabric."[136] This connectedness is important to understand because, as Jung suggested, synchronicity might have an explanatory relevance to the age-old body-soul debate through what he referred to as psychophysical parallelism.[137] Von Franz argued that the unconscious is connected to matter in a way we do not yet understand, and he suggested that synchronicity may be the mechanism through which the connection is made.[138]

Physicist Harald Atmanspacher considered two or more events that appear to be accidental or synchronistic if they exhibit the following characteristics:

- Each pair of synchronistic events includes an *internally conceived* and an *externally conceived* component.

- Any presumption of a direct *causal* relationship between the events is absurd or even inconceivable.

- The events correspond with one another by a *common meaning*, often expressed symbolically.[139]

Recognizing a synchronistic occurrence can have an important effect on us. The "aha" moment that comes from recognizing a synchronicity can be profound. Consider the following story told by Bertrand Russell in his autobiography:

> When we came home (from attending a poetry reading), we found Mrs. Whitehead undergoing an unusually severe bout of pain. She seemed cut off from everyone and everything by walls of agony, and the sense of the solitude of each human soul suddenly overwhelmed me. Ever since my marriage, my emotional life had been calm and superficial. I had forgotten all the deeper issues, and had been content with flippant cleverness. Suddenly the ground seemed to give way beneath me, and I found myself in quite another region. Within five minutes I went through some such reflection as the following: the loneliness of the human soul is unendurable; nothing can penetrate it except the highest intensity of the sort of love that religious teachers have preached; whatever does not spring from this motive is harmful, or at best useless; it follows that war is wrong, that a public school education is abominable, that the use of force is to be deprecated, and that in human relations one should penetrate to the core of loneliness in each person and speak to that...At the end of those five minutes,

I had become a completely different person. For a time, a sort of mystic illumination possessed me... Having been an imperialist, I became during those five minutes pro-Boer and a pacifist...I found myself filled with semi-mystical feelings about beauty, with an intense interest in children, and with a desire almost as profound as that of the Buddha to find some philosophy which should make human life endurable.[140]

Meaning

Meaning is important in physics, psychology, philosophy, and perhaps other fields as well; it is essential to understand what the term refers to when considering synchronicity and how synchronistic events may differ from coincidence, seriality, and serendipity. Jung recognized the difficulty in trying to convey what he meant by "meaning" in reference to synchronicity. In his essay *Synchronicity: An Acausal Connecting Principle*, he states, "What that factor which appears to us as 'meaning' may be in itself we have no possibility of knowing."[141] Jung intended meaning in this context to be an element of experience, not a formal relationship.[142]

The physicist David Bohm viewed meaning as having both mental and physical aspects. To Bohm, meaning could serve as the bridge between the inner (thoughts) and the outer (material objects). He points out that your body may very well react to that which is being perceived, as well as your consciousness.[143]

The meaning of a word or of a thing is *personal* to each of us, depending upon our own personal histories (not unlike Hume's view that words that do not bring to mind a past experience are words without meaning). Some words, such as "the" and "and" are not thought to have special meanings, but they do have definitions of which most of us are aware. Jung considered meaning to be "an element of experience, not as a formal relationship."[144]

The importance of meaning to synchronicity was introduced by the Nobel Laureate physicist Wolfgang Pauli, with whom Jung wrote his treatise on synchronicity.[145] Pauli was attempting to reconcile the objective method of physics with the subjective realm of the psyche. By including meaning in the definition of synchronicity, Jung and Pauli had developed a theory of connectedness that could be differentiated from the seriality of Kammerer.[146]

Pauli also had what I consider an extraordinary experience of synchronicity. To understand this synchronicity, it is necessary to introduce a problem that has plagued physicists: the number 137 (actually 1/137, shortened to "137"). The number was discovered in 1915 by Arnold Sommerfeld, a physicist who was Pauli's mentor, while trying to solve the "fine structure" of spectral lines, a puzzling feature of atoms. The number was "the sum of certain fundamental constants of nature, specific quantities believed to be invariable throughout the universe, quantities central to relativity, and the quantum theory." Pauli was later consumed with trying to understand why the number was what it was, because it couldn't be derived from mathematics; it was, it seemed, a "mystical number" and was referred to as such by some physicists.[147] Pauli was quoted once as saying that "if the Lord allowed him to ask anything he wanted, his first question would be 'Why 1/137?'" Perhaps Pauli had his chance. In 1958, suffering from stomach pains, he was taken to the Red Cross Hospital in Zurich. The doctors discovered massive pancreatic cancer, and he died several days later—in room 137!

Jung argued that without the reflecting consciousness of man, the world is meaningless. To Jung, synchronicity can be said to consist of two attributes: acausal orderedness and equivalent psychic and physical processes in which the observer recognizes the inherent meaning.[148] At times it seems as if Jung splits hairs in trying to defend his idea of acausality, which is a critical attribute of synchronicity. For example, in discussing the role of archetypes in synchronistic events, he argues that synchronistic events are "acts of creation in time," but they are not caused by any archetype. Archetypes merely allow the latent meaning to become perceptible.[149] However, a common definition of the term "cause" is "[t]hat which produces an effect or consequence; an antecedent or antecedents followed by a certain phenomenon."[150] By allowing "the latent meaning to become perceptible," "allowing" becomes perilously close to "causing." My point in this discussion of cause is that perhaps the term is too narrow. There may be shades of acausality, which we confuse with causality, and there may be cases of causality, which we confuse with acausality.

The general public sees meaningful coincidences as divine intervention,[151] which, in a sense, is evidence of the hidden reality. Recognizing this meaningfulness of random events has been shown to have a healing effect. For example, many alcoholics have a problem accepting one of the major tenets of Alcoholics Anonymous, which appeals to a "higher power," due to negative experiences of religion in their pasts. Mark Cameron confirmed the healing power of the experience and recognition of synchronistic events in his doctoral dissertation. His in-depth study of members of Alcoholics Anonymous showed conclusively that the spiritual development necessary for recovery from addiction is significantly enriched by the occurrence and recognition of synchronistic events.[152]

I have experienced many strange coincidences, some of which may be considered serialities and some of which qualify as synchronicities; often, the line between them is blurred. One of the strangest series of coincidences I experienced is as follows.

While completing a paper I was writing on a topic in psychology, I decided to put together some research I had on the similarities of archetypes, the unconscious, precognition, and synchronicity. I took a break from my research to complete a crossword puzzle in the local newspaper. When I had completed the puzzle, I noted that I had not entered an answer for eighteen across, which was nevertheless completed by virtue of having answered all the down clues, which provided the necessary letters. When I looked at those letters, they spelled "nixie." The clue given was "A misaddressed or illegibly addressed piece of mail." I confirmed the definition by referring to a dictionary and thought nothing more of it.

Later, I felt that it would be helpful to have Jung's book *The Archetypes and the Collective Unconscious* to aid in my research. I ordered the book from Amazon, which allowed me to begin reading it on a Kindle app. The first few pages of the book were downloaded, and I began to review them. Quite by accident I leafed to paragraph 53 (later to be found on page 25 in the book), and noted the following: "The nixie is an even more instinctive version of a magical feminine being whom I call the *anima*." This seemed a somewhat strange coincidence—seeing the word "nixie" in two different contexts within a very short time period. I made a mental note to look into it in more detail later, as I was preparing to meet my son and his friend for dinner. My son's background is in psychology, so I told him about this unusual coincidence. His friend listened to me explain what had happened and then offered that she had once owned a cat named "Nixie Knox" after a character in the Dr. Seuss book *ABC*. This additional instance of a term that I had never heard before within a period of two hours struck me as very strange.

The strange events continued. On the following Saturday, I received an email from the post office in our hometown that there was a problem with the delivery of a package to our home in Washington—misaddressed mail—a nixie! And just when I thought we had finished with this strange series of coincidences, my wife and I went to a local restaurant for breakfast the following day. Before leaving, my wife approached a young family and offered them a coupon for their breakfast since we would not be back to the restaurant before leaving town. As we were driving home, I asked her their name. She said they told her their name was Knox—yet another instance of the Nixie Knox mystery!

Was this series of coincidences an example of Jung's synchronicity or Kammerer's seriality? I could find no meaning connecting them, but the categorization of the coincidences seemed less important to me than the possibility that a hidden order was providing me evidence of its existence. These coincidences seemed, in some not-understood way, connected. Perhaps the statistical improbability of the series of events was so great that the recognition of that improbability was, in itself, a special kind of meaning.[153]

The differences between the terms used to describe the relationship between two or more events may be artificial. We are using the words available to us in our native language, a language that may be wholly inadequate to the task, such as when we try to translate the word "serendipity." Jung noted this in a 1929 lecture in which he stated, "Synchronicism is the prejudice of the East, causality is the modern prejudice of the West."[154] Perhaps a better way to understand the relationship between two or more events will be found in a middle ground between those two prejudices.

When we experience coincidences that seem to have no causal relationship, we should consider the possibility that there may be a hidden order underlying reality, which explains the connection between the events without the need to categorize the connection as either "synchronicity" or "seriality."

4

Misconceptions of Evolutionary Theory

D'où Venons Nous

It is difficult to get a man to understand something, when his salary depends on his not understanding it.
—Upton Sinclair

It is absurd for the Evolutionist to complain that it is unthinkable for an admittedly unthinkable God to make everything out of nothing, and then pretend that it is more thinkable that nothing should turn itself into everything.
—G. K. Chesterton

Darwin never really did discuss the origin of species in his *On the Origin of Species.*
—Ernst Mayr

> If evolution is to work smoothly, consciousness in
> some shape must have been present at the very ori-
> gin of things.
> —William James

> Nothing new comes into the world by evolution,
> there comes only the development, the unfolding
> of what was there.
> —G. T. Fechner

SCIENTISTS HAVE CONSTRUCTED A THEORY of where we come from by relying on the idea of evolution. Evolution is a broad term used in the sciences of cosmology, chemistry, and biology to explain how one "thing" changes into another "thing."[155] Evolution, however, is not simply "change"—it denotes "transformation."[156] Cosmological evolution seeks to explain how solar systems arise from stars, stars from galaxies, galaxies from galactic clusters, and galactic clusters from the universe.[157] Biological evolution refers to the gradual conversion of organisms from one or more common precursors, progressing from single cells to invertebrates, including animals and plants, to fish, to amphibians, to reptiles, to birds, to lower mammals, to primates, and finally, to humans. Chemical evolution begins with the transformation to life from nonlife.

Evolution may not explain the origin of the universe or organic life, but it may apply to something as intangible as the laws of nature. Sheldrake notes that the idea of there being "laws of nature" is metaphorical in that it is based on an analogy with laws established by humans, which are rules of conduct.[158] Perhaps the "laws of nature" have "evolved," and that may explain our inability to understand how the universe and life came into existence: we are trying to understand those mysteries given the "laws of nature" that we now have.

Cosmological Evolution

One theory of how the universe began is referred to as the big bang theory. The big bang theory, Carl Sagan explained, holds that the universe was "created, *somehow*, ten or twenty billion years ago and expands forever [my italics]."[159] Notably, Sagan is not suggesting that the universe "evolved"; he is acknowledging that the universe was *created*. An alternate theory favored by Sagan is that the universe "has no beginning and no end, and we are in the midst of an infinite cycle of cosmic deaths and rebirths."[160] No proof has been offered as to which theory, if either, is true, so it's fair to say that the beginning of the universe remains a mystery. One thing we can say with a degree of confidence is that the beginning of the universe did not "evolve," for evolution, as I explained, involves transformation, and that implies that there was something to be transformed. The question of how the universe began is clearly beyond our ability to know with any degree of certainty.

Cooper notes that just for our planet, "At least six cosmic parameters have to be so finely tuned that the overall tolerances cannot vary by more than 1 in 10,"[200] which is an unimaginably small number.[161] Einstein taught us that matter can be created out of energy, and energy out of matter, but this leaves unanswered the question of from where either the energy or the matter arose. Simply put, you cannot create something out of nothing. Those who argue against intelligent design seem to omit the fact that evolution can only apply if something already exists, which can then evolve.

Biological Evolution

The existence of life is a truly miraculous process, and Darwinists' attempts to "shoehorn" this process into a materialist paradigm fails. Even some of the most ardent materialists recognize the obvious appearance of design with purpose, from the beginning of the universe to the rise of organic life, but ironically deny that the *appearance* of design is, in fact, the result of design. Richard Dawkins, a faithful defender of neo-Darwinism, has stated, "[T]he living results of natural selection overwhelmingly impress us with the illusion of design and planning."[162]

In 1966 a scientific conference was held at the Wistar Institute of Anatomy and Biology, in which some of the most distinguished evolutionary scientists were present. The reasons for the gathering were explained by Sir Peter Medawar of the National Institute for Medical Research in London, England:

> The immediate cause of this conference is a pretty widespread sense of *dissatisfaction* about what has come to be thought of as the accepted evolutionary theory in the English-speaking world, the so-called neo-Darwinian Theory…These objections to current neo-Darwinian theory *are very widely held among biologists generally*; and we must on no account, I think, make light of them. The very fact that we are having this conference is evidence that we are not making light of them.[163]

One of the problems with Darwinism is that it is little more than a tautology providing no real predictive or explanatory power. A "tautology" is an expression or phrase that says the same thing twice. Professor Murray Eden of MIT, who was in attendance at the conference mentioned above, considered neo-Darwinism's adaptation of species to be just that:

> As an instance, the statement that species *adapt* to changes in an environment by a variation in the properties of the phenotypes and by the consequent process of natural selection is clearly *vacuous*...Since these are the only possibilities, the original statement is *tautologous*.[164]

Darwin's theory consists primarily of two ideas: variation through small, inherited changes and natural selection. The small variations to which Darwin gave credit are those that, he argued, occur randomly. Natural selection is the result of those randomly occurring variations adding to the organism's ability to survive and reproduce. However, contrary to Darwin's gradualism, it has been well established that species typically appear abruptly. The curator of the University Museum at Oxford has stated, "Most fossil species appear instantaneously... persist for millions of years virtually unchanged, only to disappear abruptly."[165] Additionally, it was stated that "it is not always clear, in fact it's rarely clear, that the descendants were actually better adapted than their predecessors. In other words, biological improvement is hard to find."[166] If there is no good evidence to show that evolution as conceived by Darwin has "improved" the species, then what validity does Darwin's evolutionary theory have?

The sudden appearance of groups of species was a problem that Darwin recognized in *On the Origin of Species*. Darwin made a statement in his text that raises major questions: "If numerous species, belonging to the same genera or families, have really started into life at once, the fact would be fatal to the theory of evolution through natural selection."[167] He also recognized that the fossil record did not support his theories. He stated:

> To the question why we do not find rich fossilifer-
> ous deposits belonging to these assumed earliest
> periods prior to the Cambrian system, I can give
> no satisfactory answer...The case at present must
> remain inexplicable; and may truly be urged as a
> valid argument against the views here entertained.[168]

Darwin's original thesis claimed that "all the organic beings which have ever lived on this earth descended from some one primordial form."[169] Somewhat ironically, he never explained *how life originated* in his book *On the Origin of Species*. His claim of a common ancestor failed to explain the nature or the origin of that common ancestor. This glaring absence of any explanation as to how life originated was widely criticized, even by his supporters.[170] Furthermore, as I explained above, evolution involves transformation: there had to be something that existed at the beginning of the evolutionary process that was subject to the change and transformation. Evolution is silent on the question of from where or how that "something" arose.[171]

J. B. S. Haldane, a British-Indian scientist, tried to elaborate on how life began in a paper published in 1929. He presented his hypothesis that the origin of life consisted of three main stages: "Firstly, organic molecules were synthesized under the action of ultra-violet on a primordial mixture of water, carbon dioxide, and ammonia. Secondly, under the action of the sun's radiation on this hot dilute soup, large molecules capable to reproduce themselves emerged. Thirdly, cells were formed."[172] New research, however, rejects Haldane's hypothesis altogether.[173]

The idea of all organic life arising from a single primordial source is merely a theory that lacks supporting evidence. In fact, the evidence that does exist is in conflict with Darwin's original idea. W. R. Bird, the author of a text critical of Darwin, notes "Actually we shall never be able to prove the common ancestry of all animals, and therefore we have no right to state as a fundamental principle what must always remain an assumption."[174]

Why Darwinian evolutionary theory is considered *sacrosanct*—a term that certainly does not belong in any scientific investigation—is mystery. The Darwinian paradigm is so rigid that alternative theories and those who propose them are looked upon with scorn by mainstream science.

A case in point is described by Bird. A Chinese paleontologist, J. Y. Chen, discovered many early Cambrian life forms. He had published numerous scientific papers on the find, which supported earlier research, but which showed that "the Cambrian [period] animals appeared even more explosively than previously realized."[175] In a 2000 lecture at the University of Washington, he emphasized the contradictions between China's fossil evidence and the accepted Darwinian dogma. "As a result, one professor in the audience asked Chen, almost as if in warning, if he wasn't nervous about expressing his doubts about Darwinism so freely [Chen's reply was] In China… we can criticize Darwin, but not the government. In America, you can criticize the government, but not Darwin."[176] Professor Chen's observation exemplifies the difficulty in challenging the existing evolutionary theory paradigm.

In spite of these evidential problems with the theory, it boasts wide support among many scientists, irrespective of the fact that it cannot be shown to be true through application of the scientific method, and for that reason remains merely a theory.[177, 178] It is notable, and to their credit, that some philosophers and scientists who consider themselves "anti-Darwinist" are able to acknowledge the possible truth of some of what Darwin argued while challenging other parts of the theory that don't hold up under scrutiny. For example, Fodor and Piattelli-Palmarini began their analysis of the problems of Darwinism with the following statement:

> The (neo-)Darwinian theory of evolution...has two distinct but related parts: there's a historical account of the genealogy of species...and there's the theory of natural selection...The main thesis of this book is that [natural selection] is irredeemably flawed. However, we have no quarrel to pick with genealogy of species; it is perfectly possible—in fact, entirely likely—that [genealogy of species] is true even if [natural selection] is not.[179]

Strict Darwinian evolutionary theory has matured into neo-Darwinism, which is simply a blend of Darwin's ideas with those of Gregor Mendel, a contemporary of Darwin and a pioneer in the field of genetics. Neo-Darwinian theory attempted to modernize Darwinian theory by incorporating a view of heredity that is explainable in terms of genes and chromosomes; however, it steadfastly clings to the Darwinian idea that those heritable variables are attributable to the random mutation of genetic material.[180] In other words, to the neo-Darwinist, evolution is a purely random event but one that results in mutation and recombination of genetic material. The random mutation and recombination is believed to result in genetic changes in children which differ from that of either parent.

It is notable that both the absence of evidence of "gradual changes" and the failure to show improvement in the progeny have nonetheless failed to persuade Darwinian loyalists to acknowledge that the theory does not accord with the evidence. Another criticism of Darwin's theory is that it argues that as time passes, there are higher levels of organization in determinate structures and functions. This view is in conflict with classical thermodynamic theory, which maintains that as time progresses, there is movement toward states of *disorganization*.[181] Just as controversial as the absences in the fossil record are the sudden disappearances of some species. Stephen Meyer, a Cambridge PhD, asks, "Where in the Ordovician strata, for instance, are many of the families of the trilobites and brachiopods present in the Cambrian just below it? These creatures along with numerous other types suddenly disappear."[182] Although neo-Darwinism is the theory du jour of a large number of scientists, it fails to address these deficiencies and others.

There is a common argument made by Darwinists that even when there are significant gaps in the fossil record, it does not prove evolution is wrong. In Chapter 2, I introduced the argument "absence of evidence isn't evidence of absence" to show how a physicist's argument against the future discovery of new forces or particles was faulty. However, when a credible professional argues that intelligent design is a possible explanation for the creation of life, that professional is not "permitted" to use the "absence of evidence is not evidence of absence" argument.

Additionally, since the Darwinian idea that all living organisms evolved from the same "primordial soup" begins with an assumption of the existence of some primordial material that has not been shown to have existed—the argument is faulty. For an argument to be sound, its premise must be true, and the truth of the premise used in the argument for evolution has not been shown to be true.

Huston Smith was a widely recognized religious scholar who also noted the problems with beginning an argument on an unproven footing. He noted four problems with the idea of big bang culminating in intelligent beings in the span of twenty billion years. First, he notes that Allan Sandage of the Observatories of the Carnegie Institution "recently proposed that the 'Big Bang' could only be understood as 'a miracle,' in which some higher force must have played a role." Second, if one assumes the big bang did occur, the question arises as to how matter arose from nonmatter. This is the same logic problem discussed above. You can have a valid argument, but if you begin with unproven hypotheses, "you're lost." Third, there is the unsolved question as to how qualities arise from quantities: "The world comes to us clothed in sounds and colors and fragrances, which in textbook science have no right to be there." And finally, if we conflate the brain with the mind, there is the question as to how thoughts and feelings arise.[183]

I also consider the arguments put forth by neo-Darwinian theorists to be a classic example of the "red herring" fallacy, which attempts to divert attention from the real issue, which is the miracle of existence QED.

Consider this metaphor: if you were to see a magic show in which a magician places a small amount of "primordial goo" on the table, covers it with a cloth, says a few words, waves a wand, and presto, a human being appears, you would most likely consider that real magic or a miracle. Intelligent design theorists recognize not only the miraculous transformation of "primordial goo" into a human being, but the miracle of the very existence of the "goo." Neo-Darwinians want to know what went on under the cloth—they look to the steps and the time factor to explain the miracle. In so doing, they are missing the real magic: the fact that a human was created. There is something even more magical and miraculous than starting from primordial goo…and that is the creation of the primordial goo; for something like even the very basic "primordial goo" to appear requires a miracle in itself—a miracle created by intelligent design.

This metaphor illustrates what I consider to be the true problem in the debates over whether we and the universe came about through evolution, intelligent design, or creationism. We do not have to fully understand how the magician was able to create a human from a small vial of "primordial goo" (or even better, to create a human from nothing!) to appreciate and acknowledge that what we saw happen on stage was truly a miracle. Neo-Darwinian evolutionary theory argues that the same feat was accomplished over millions of years. That theory attempts to draw our attention to what may have happened under the sheet, focusing on the processes that Darwinists presume are occurring. The "intelligent design" theorist sees the miracle that occurred. But what are the real differences, except the intermediate steps and the variable of time? If the magician's feat is seen as a miracle, how is it less than a miracle if it took millions of years or millions of intermediate steps? The fact that the universe and all life exists is a miracle no different than the feat of a stage magician, save for the time it takes and the steps taken under each of the two scenarios. My point is that, except for the factor of time, the theories of evolution and intelligent design are not as disparate as they appear; the relevant distinction between the two arguments has to do with the source of the so-called "primordial goo."

You may wonder why a book titled *Ultimate Reality: A Challenge to the Materialist Paradigm* would include a discussion on evolution. There are at least four reasons. First, the polemics between Darwinists and intelligent design theorists detract from the real mystery, which is the fact that everything in the universe does exist and came from somewhere we cannot identify with certainty. Secondly, the weaknesses in neo-Darwinian theory give evidence of intelligent design. Thirdly, if, as the evidence indicates, the universe was designed, then there is a designer. Fourthly, if there is a designer, that implies that there is a purpose for the design.

Some years ago I read Michael Cremo's *Forbidden Archeology*, which strengthened my suspicions that the accepted theory of how humans came to be was problematic. In his book, Cremo cites archeological evidence from published reports by experts in their fields, which suggests that humans may have existed before, and even coexisted with, other primates. Cremo's research was funded by a Vedic organization, and as a result, it has been vehemently attacked and referred to as a "pseudoarcheological" work: "[S]cholars of mainstream archeology and paleo-anthropology have gone so far as to describe it as pseudoscience."[184] Regardless of the attacks on the work, I consider Cremo to be a credible researcher who was willing to explore ideas outside existing paradigms and withstand the ad hominem attacks that were sure to follow.

Cremo sent a copy of his book to William W. Howells, emeritus professor of physical anthropology at Harvard University, who considered its thesis thoughtfully and responded with the following statement:

> Thank you for sending me a copy of *Forbidden Archeology*, which represents much careful effort in critically assembling published materials. I have given it a good examination…Most of us, mistakenly or

not, see human evolution as a succession of branchings from earlier to more advanced forms of primate, with man emerging rather late…To have modern human beings…appearing a great deal earlier, in fact at a time when even simple primates did not exist as possible ancestors, would be devastating not only to the accepted pattern. It would be devastating to the whole theory of evolution… The suggested hypothesis would demand a kind of process which could not possibly be accommodated by evolutionary theory as we know it, and I should think it requires an explanation.[185]

Intelligent Design

Intelligent design is a theory that argues that the universe was designed by an unidentified source. In a twist of irony, it is considered to be nonscientific because it cannot be empirically tested. This criticism of intelligent design also applies to creationism. It is notable that Darwinists attack intelligent design as not being verifiable through the rigors of the scientific method; however, the theories of Darwinists are also not scientifically testable. There is no proof of any kind that supports the notion that one species can become another species, even given extremely long time periods. Darwin's treatise *On the Origin of Species* never did offer a definitive explanation of how new species arise, or for that matter, how life arose. I suggest this should be the major focus of the arguments between those who argue an intelligent designer created the universe and all that is in it and neo-Darwinists, who start their argument with the "primordial goo." Where and how did the "primordial goo," the *prima materia*, originate? Darwin leaves that question unanswered. What is of interest in comparing the theories of neo-Darwinism, intelligent design, and creationism is that in a strict scientific sense, none of those theories can claim to explain the origin of life through the application of the scientific method, which requires observation, measurement, testing, and modification of the hypotheses as required.

Karl Popper, one of the preeminent philosophers of science, stated on the subject of evolution: "It is metaphysical because it is not testable."[186] If Popper is correct that evolution is a "metaphysical" theory and not scientific (because it doesn't meet Popper's "testability-falsifiability" requirement), why aren't more scientists open to at least considering the idea that intelligent design is as feasible an explanation as evolution? To answer that question, we need only refer to Planck's comment in Chapter 1 that paradigms change when opponents to the new ideas die off and those who grew up with the idea come to the fore. The old scientists who are trapped in the materialist paradigm, such as Dawkins, may have to die off before there is any substantive receptivity to intelligent design as a possible explanation.

In an attempt to support his attack on the theory of intelligent design, Dawkins programmed a computer to generate sequences of English letters, presumably to show how random mutations coupled with natural selection would create new information. However, as noted by Meyer, Dawkins ignored the fact that behind this computer program running these simulations was an intelligent designer: Richard Dawkins, who had programmed the computer! This seems to be a recurring theme in the arguments of neo-Darwinians. They bring elements of design into their defense of evolution. Meyer notes that "Dawkins repeatedly smuggled in the very thing he insisted the concept of natural selection expressly precluded: the guiding hand of an intelligent agent."[187]

To further illustrate how Dawkins misses the forest by scrutinizing the bark of a tree with a magnifying glass, consider his observation on the possibility of the haemoglobin [British spelling]. He considers the creation of the haemoglobin purely by chance to be impossible:

> The number we seek, the "haemoglobin number," is (near enough) a 1 with 190 noughts [zeros] after it! This is the chance against happening to hit upon a haemoglobin by luck. And a haemoglobin molecule has only a minute fraction of the complexity of a living body."[188]

How, one may ask, does the impossibility of the random creation by chance of a haemoglobin support Dawkins's argument in support of Darwinian theory? This is, to me, a mystery in itself. It seems much better suited to support an argument for intelligent design.

Dawkins, when confronted with questions about how we come to be, punts them to other disciplines such as physics.[189] He steadfastly refuses to see the attraction of intelligent design because his career and reputation have been built on Darwinian theory. It is as though he is locked in a paradigm for which he sees no exit nor any need for an exit. Imagine what would happen if he were to show sympathy to any criticism of Darwinian evolution. Upton Sinclair, quoted at the beginning of this chapter, may help us understand: "It is difficult to get a man to understand something, when his salary depends on his not understanding it." This is a clear example of a closed mind, which is indefensible in what should be an unbiased search for truth.

Teleology

Teleology is considered "[t]he argument for the existence of God from the evidence of order, and hence design, in nature."[190] Lennox makes the surprising claim that Darwin was, in fact, a teleologist:

> In order to assess whether Darwin's version of evolutionary theory does or does not employ Teleological explanation, two of his botanical studies are examined. The result of this examination is that Darwin sees selection explanations of adaptations as teleological explanations.[191]

Lennox supports his argument by reference to an assertion made by Asa Gray, a contemporary of Darwin who had commented, "Darwin's great service to Natural Science in bringing back to it Teleology: so that instead of Morphology versus Teleology, we shall have Morphology wedded to Teleology." Darwin responded to this comment by stating, "What you say about Teleology pleases me especially and I do not think anyone else has ever noticed the point."[192] Can Lennox's article showing how Darwin accepted the label of teleologist, albeit without a philosophical commentary on the meaning of the word, give us insight into what Darwin actually thought of intelligent design?

In an essay, Mayr provides us with a comprehensive discussion on *The Multiple Meanings of Teleological*, stating, "If *teleological* means anything, it means *goal-directed*."[193] The question of what Darwin meant by "teleological" and what Mayr and others claim he meant is the subject of debate. Mayr assures us Darwin felt that teleonomic processes involving a single individual were materially different from those involving evolutionary changes.[194] What I find interesting is how some writers work so diligently to try to explain away any questions Darwin may have had concerning goal-directed evolutionary processes. We will never know with certainty Darwin's view of teleology or goal-directed evolutionary processes. However, Mayr acknowledges that in his later years, Darwin referred to "the extreme difficulty or rather impossibility of conceiving of this immense and wonderful universe, including man with his capacity for looking far backwards and far into futurity, as the result of blind chance or necessity."[195]

Perhaps Darwinism can be likened to a religion. The English biologist William Bateson remarked, "We have the impression that it is only by extraordinary acts of faith that biologists can suppose that the actual progress of life can be explained in the terms they adopt."[196] "Faith," as I pointed out in Chapter 1, can be thought of as a confident *belief* in the truth, value, or trustworthiness of a person, idea, or thing. It is not, however, itself considered trustworthy.

Lamarckism

Lamarckism, in contrast to neo-Darwinism, is a theory based upon the work of Jean-Baptiste Lamarck during the nineteenth century. His theory of evolution was built upon the idea that physical changes in an organism during its lifetime could be transmitted to its offspring. He argued that as animals moved into new environments, they experienced new needs for which they developed new habits, leading to greater use of some organs and a decline in the use of other organs. The changes so acquired were passed on to succeeding generations.[197] Lamarck's theory has been largely discredited by adherents to the neo-Darwinian paradigm, although there have been experiments that seem to show it has some validity. For example, an experiment conducted at McGill University in Montreal showed that by teaching mice to fear an odor, their offspring and the next generation of their offspring are born with a fear of it.[198] Furthermore, Lamarckian theory seems to explain why camels have callosities on their knees, which protect them when they kneel. Sheldrake notes that one can understand how these develop in response to abrasions, but baby camels are born with them.[199] Meyer also notes that "more biologists have recognized that some biological information-epigenetic information [heritable changes that do not involve changes in the DNA sequence] resides in structures outside of DNA."[200] In an article in *Nature* (1964), Dr. J. Bristol Foster addressed the evolution of mammals on islands, concluding:

> However, it can clearly be shown that insularity [living or located on an island] has been a major force in the evolution of the forms and has been underrated in similar work in the past...If it is possible to imagine the advantages of rodents becoming larger on islands, one must still explain why larger mammals (carnivores, lagomorphs and artiodactyls) usually become smaller.[201]

This work on insularity and the size of mammals suggests evidence of Lamarckism: the changing size of animals was influenced by the environment, not by random variations.

Koonin and Wolf looked at the possibility that Lamarckian theory might have relevance in assessing the role of evolution, noting that "various evolutionary phenomena that came to the fore in the last few years, seem to fit a more broadly interpreted (quasi) Lamarckian paradigm," ultimately concluding that "[b]oth Darwinian and Lamarckian modalities of evolution appear to be important, and reflect different aspects of the interaction between populations and the environment."[202] It is also noteworthy that Darwin himself did not rule out the idea of inheritance of acquired characteristics.[203]

Geneticist Richard Goldschmidt, credited with being the first to try to integrate genetics, development, and evolution, made the following comment concerning Lamarckism before it was so widely renounced:

> It is well worth while to enquire whether such an evolution can possibly have taken place on Darwinian lines. How the woodpecker or stone crusher [a bird] type, which involves, of course, the whole anatomy, may have evolved from a honey-sucker type by a series of micro-mutations controlled by selection is simply unimaginable, and one can understand why so many geneticists stick to the Lamarckian explanation...We cannot understand either, why all these different lines of evolution should have blossomed out simultaneously, even if a neo-Darwinian interpretation of the resulting type were feasible.[204]

Forms

Forms are one more hurdle for materialist reliance on the role biology plays in creating living organisms: "The forms of all but the simplest systems can only be represented visually, whether by photographs, drawings, diagrams or models. They cannot be represented mathematically."[205] The form an organism exhibits cannot be reduced to chemical molecules or physical quantities. Sheldrake explains:

> The coming-into-being of the form of an organism—its *morphogenesis* certainly involves numerous

chemical and physical changes, and the expenditure
of measurable quantities of energy. So does its behaviour. But neither morphogenesis nor behaviour
bears the same immediate relation to chemistry as
do molecules studied by biochemists and molecular
biologists, or to physics as the physical processes
studied by biophysicists and electrophysiologists.
It is at this point the mechanistic theory runs into
serious difficulties.[206]

Clearly, if we do not know how "forms" in the broadest sense
arise, then it presents problems for natural selection being considered
the sole instrument of change in biological systems. If the argument
from design is credible, and there are a growing number of scientists
and philosophers who are willing to consider that possibility, then
one must further consider the possibility that we and the universe
were designed for a purpose. Whether one calls the designer God,
ultimate reality, or universal intelligence, the fact remains: if we were
designed, there must be a purpose—or else why bother? Why is evolution such an important topic in this book? It is because historically
the dogma of evolutionary theory has been used to repudiate the
idea of an intelligent designer (i.e., God). And as I have made clear
throughout this book, and in agreement with religious scholar Huston
Smith, God and "ultimate reality" are one and the same. If intelligent
design can be shown to be an acceptable alternative to evolutionary
theory—and I think it can be—then there must have been an intelligent designer: God. Ultimate reality is another name, albeit a less
contentious one, for God. And once the existence of the spiritual,
nonmaterialist ultimate reality is accepted, the possible existence of
a spiritual, nonmaterialist component of the Self becomes axiomatic.

Sheldrake refers to Occam's razor in rebuttal to materialist's preference for a multiverse explanation for creation. The argument is that even though the odds of the universe we inhabit having been created randomly are infinitesimally small, the infinity of parallel universes (as postulated in quantum theory), increases the chance that we just happen to be existing in the "right one for us." Occam's razor holds that "entities should not be multiplied without necessity." To materialists and neo-Darwinists, it is no violation of Occam's razor to posit multiple universes. Given that there is no proof at all that there are multiple universes, why would a scientist be willing to advance a theory to support his views, for which there is no evidence, and be unwilling to consider the idea of intelligent design, for which there is much evidence? Sheldrake notes that "invoking billions of unobserved universes does not even succeed in getting rid of God [or an intelligent designer]. An infinite God could be the God of an infinite number of universes."[207] And so it goes…round and round with seemingly no common ground between the two camps. Hopefully, my metaphor of the stage magician shows that the very fact that we and the universe are here, at least in the perceptual reality, is evidence of something miraculous.

Donald Hoffman is a professor of cognitive science who argues that we do not see the ultimate reality because of evolution. He offers an interesting metaphor involving the icons on a computer desktop. When we look at an icon on our computer, we don't see "transistors, voltages, magnetic fields, logic gates, binary codes, and gigabytes of software…The language of the interface—pixels and icons—cannot describe the hardware and software it hides."[208] His theory, called the interface theory of perception (ITP), argues that ultimate reality is hidden from our perception in the same way icons on a computer desktop hide what is going in the programs and apps represented by the icons. Furthermore, Hoffman attributes that to evolution, claiming that evolution

> has endowed us with senses that hide the truth and display the simple icons we need to survive long enough to raise our offspring. Space as your perceive it when you look around, is just your desktop—a 3D desktop. Apples, snakes, and other physical objects are simply icons in your 3D desktop.[209]

I find Hoffman's metaphor to be a good one, but his reliance on Darwin to support his theory is problematic: the existence of the "icons" may have been there at creation; they may be part of the design at the beginning, not something that evolved. There are no examples from the fossil record of animals that saw ultimate reality other than as icons, and that were thereby headed for extinction.

He introduces another acronym: fitness beats truth (FBT), which he claims is a result of natural selection. He argues that natural selection "favors perceptions that assist us in scoring fitness points. If the number of fitness points happen to correlate with a structure in the world, such as the amount of stuf [*sic*], then evolution will happen to favor *Truth*." The point Hoffman is making is that evolution favors the perception of fitness, not of truth. Thus, a creature that sees behind the doors of perception and perceives ultimate reality will miss the lion coming up behind him.[210]

In support of Hoffman's argument, I would prefer to be wandering in the jungle with a materialist rather than a poet or an artist who might be enjoying the beauty of their surroundings unaware of the threats that exist. The sensibilities that the creature needs to perceive the "icon" will enable it to survive and reproduce. But why, one may ask, does Hoffman find it necessary to invoke natural selection to support his theory? Perhaps it is because the theory of natural selection has been described as one that "with a little ingenuity *any observation* can be made to appear consistent with" (my emphasis).[211] Hoffman's theory of FBT suffers from the same fault as Darwin's theory of survival of the fittest: it is tautologous. Creatures who fail the "fitness beats truth" test don't survive; ergo, all the creatures who survived passed the fitness test.

To understand what is behind Hoffman's "icons" requires daring to consider the spiritual nature of reality and what may lie beyond the doors of perception. That may not save you from the lions, but if you are successful, you will have experienced the ineffable mystery of ultimate reality, and to some of us, that is worth a lot.

I leave this chapter with the following quote from Professor Waddington, whom Koestler unceremoniously referred to as a "quasi-Trotskyite":

> To suppose that the evolution of the wonderfully adapted biological mechanisms has depended only on a selection out of a haphazard set of variations, each produced by blind chance, is like suggesting that if we went on throwing bricks together in heaps, we should eventually be able to choose ourselves the most desirable house.[212]

5

The Ubiquity of Consciousness

Que Sommes Nous

THE FIRST STEP TO ANSWER Gauguin's question "What are we?" is to understand what it means to be conscious. That turns out to be more difficult than it sounds.

"Nobody has the faintest idea what consciousness is...I don't have any idea. Nor does anybody else, including the philosophers of mind."[213] This quote by Stuart Kauffman, a theoretical biologist and complex theorist, sounds like that of Richard Feynman, who confessed the same lack of understanding about quantum physics, discussed earlier.[214]

Solving the riddle of consciousness is going to require the acceptance of a spiritual, nonphysical dimension. Consciousness did not just come into being through evolution—it came about from an unfolding of what was already in existence.[215] It is a manifestation of an ultimate reality that embodies universal intelligence. Max Planck, a Nobel physicist, had this to say about the existence of a mind operating behind all matter:

As a man who has devoted his whole life to the most clearheaded science, to the study of matter, I can tell you as a result of my research about the atoms this much: There is no matter as such! All matter originates and exists only by virtue of a force which brings the particles of an atom to vibration and holds this most minute solar system of the atom together...We must assume behind this force the existence of a conscious and intelligent Mind. This Mind is the matrix of all matter.[216]

One who professes a material realism view of consciousness and the mind is John Searle, a philosopher of the mind. Searle is, however, honest in his recognition of the problems inherent in the materialist paradigm when it comes to the problem of body, mind, and consciousness. He has stated,

Acceptance of the current views is motivated not so much by an independent conviction of their truth as by a terror of what are apparently the only alternatives. That is, the choice we are tacitly presented with is between a "scientific" approach, as represented by one or another of the current versions of "materialism," and an "anti-scientific" approach, as represented by Cartesianism or some other traditional religious conception of the mind.[217]

Searle's comment exemplifies the reluctance of mainstream scientists to consider any approach to the mystery of mind that might involve anything spiritual or nonmaterial.

Dossey, Greyson, Sturrock, and Tucker try to solve the problem of consciousness by postulating that there are two different types of science: Type I science and Type II science.[218] Type I science is a discipline in which one begins with agreed-upon concepts—an established knowledge base—and then explores the consequences. Most science operates on these principles. In contrast, Type II science is an inductive process that begins with phenomena that are not understood, and that lack useful concepts on which to rely. Quantum physics would be an example of a Type II science. Eugene Wigner, whom I mentioned earlier, recognized the problem with trying to understand the nature of consciousness by the use of Type 1 science: "It [physics] will have to be replaced by new laws, based upon new concepts, if organisms with consciousness are to be described. [I]n order to deal with the phenomenon of life, the laws of physics will have to be changed, not only reinterpreted."[219]

There are three theories of consciousness that I want to discuss. They are epiphenomenalism, emergentism, and panpsychism. Although each one of these theories has variations, I will limit the discussion to the main points.

Epiphenomenalism

"Epiphenomenalism" holds that consciousness is solely a property of the brain. That is the view of material realists.[220] An argument that materialists employ to reinforce their position that the brain is the mind revolves around the problem of how a physical brain could interact with an immaterial mind. Epiphenomenalists argue that there is no acceptable theory as to how such interaction could occur [recall the "absence of evidence" argument in Chapter 2]. Although I find the epiphenomenalist argument unconvincing on its face, it is also naive in its failure to see how a brain and a mind could interact. There is an analogous situation where a stone, a material object, interacts with an immaterial force such as gravity. Quantum physics also gives examples in the phenomena of wave-particle duality and entanglement. In quantum physics, the immaterial gaze of a spectator can cause an immaterial wave to collapse into a material particle: "All matter exhibits this curious mixture of wave and particle character and the uncertainty principle describes the relationship between these two complementary properties."[221] Niels Bohr, who won a Nobel Prize for his contributions to quantum theory, concluded that there was no underlying physical reality existing independently of a measuring apparatus. A number of quantum physicists agree.[222] If there is no "underlying physical reality," then the problem of how a "material brain" interacts with an "immaterial mind" becomes inconsequential.

If consciousness is not an epiphenomenon, then the question arises as to how consciousness and the body are related. Two distinctly different schools of thought on how consciousness arose are emergentism and panpsychism.[223]

Benjamin Libet was a researcher in the physiology department at UCSF. He did pioneering research into human consciousness, proposing some revolutionary ideas as to how the brain and consciousness interact. His research showed that the brain registers the decision to make movements before a person consciously decides to move.[224] This indicates that there was a time delay between the time the physical reaction was recorded in the brain and when the person made a conscious decision to move. Some critics have argued that his experiment was flawed, others that it proves the myth of free will. More importantly, for purposes of this discussion, Libet's experiment reinforces the argument that consciousness is "not the brain." If consciousness is the brain, as has been argued by some, then there would be no difference in time between the conscious decision to move and the brain's registering of that decision. Libet felt that his experiments with the delay between conscious awareness of the desire to act and the actual movement were evidence of a conscious mental field (CMF).[225]

Emergentism

The theory of emergentism holds that the mind "emerged" at some point in evolutionary history. Most philosophers of the mind argue that the mind emerged from matter, but they are unable to explain how such emergence is possible.[226] The case for emergentism is weak and in conflict with what quantum physics seems to be telling us. Science is unable to explain how life began, and the same holds true for consciousness. In a twist of irony, many of the scientists who argue that life cannot arise from nonlife paradoxically argue that mind can arise from nonmind. Generally, those who believe emergentism explains consciousness take the position that although consciousness is not physical, it is not completely independent of the physical. They are trying to finesse a position between "'crass reductionism' on the one hand and 'spooky dualism' on the other."[227]

Panpsychism

Panpsychism is the view that every "thing" that exists in space-time has a mental element. The doctrine of panpsychism has appeal to those who feel that the immaterial mind cannot have arisen from nonmental, material things as emergentists believe.[228] The difficulty in accepting the theory of panpsychism for some comes from its core principle that everything has a mental element. Nevertheless, it does have credible supporters.

Generally, those who adhere to the theory of emergentism are materialists. However, since emergentism has the problem of explaining how consciousness "emerged" into the material brain, some materialists have become sympathetic to the panpsychist theory that perhaps electrons have some rudimentary form of consciousness. They are then able to argue that the brain is the coordinating organ for the rudimentary consciousness of the subatomic electrons. This acceptance of a very narrow view of panpsychism is an attempt to reinforce the materialist paradigm, while avoiding the question as to whether the universe and everything in it is truly conscious, and not just with "some rudimentary form of consciousness."

Perhaps an even more important question than the consciousness of electrons is, How do I know you are conscious? Although I can only know my own consciousness with certainty, I believe that you and all human beings are conscious. To doubt that others possess consciousness is called "solipsism." A solipsist is one who is only confident in their own conscious existence. As one moves away from solipsism, it becomes easier to consider the possibility that consciousness, in some rudimentary form, pervades all matter. This does not mean, for example, that rocks are conscious or possess a mind—only that the rocks' most basic subatomic parts have mental aspects.[229] While there is no evidence supporting the idea that inanimate objects such as stones have a mental life, it is possible that the subatomic particles that comprise inanimate matter do.

Christof Koch, the chief scientific officer at the Allen Institute for Brain Science in Seattle, holds that "panpsychism is an elegant explanation for the most basic of all brute facts."[230] Panpsychism offers a convenient way to avoid the major problem with materialism by making the claim that consciousness is a basic attribute of all matter: there is no need to explain how it "enters" matter—it's there at creation. Werner Heisenberg, who received the Nobel Prize in physics for the creation of quantum physics, believed that some sort of consciousness may exist in even the most simple of organisms. Physicist Menas Kafatos and alternative medicine advocate Dr. Deepak Chopra claim that "[c]onsciousness and matter are not fundamentally distinct but rather are two complementary aspects of one reality, embracing the micro and macro worlds."[231] This "one reality" is comprised of both the reality of our perception and the hidden reality that manifests in that perceptual reality in ways I have described. The claim that consciousness and matter are complementary aspects of one reality is not popular in the scientific community.

Eastern Philosophy of Consciousness
Indian philosophy departs from the Western philosophical idea that there is but "one consciousness." An Indian identifies four states of consciousness: the waking state, the dream state, the state of dreamless sleep, and a fourth state that is simply referred to as "the fourth." It should also be noted that to an Indian, in the state of dreamless sleep, we are more aware than when we are awake or dreaming.[232]

Buddhist philosophy, in contrast to Indian philosophy, has no universally accepted view on the subject of consciousness. Buddhism is a plural tradition that has a variety of views about the mind that have evolved over the centuries.[233]

Sentience
In the debate on the nature and ubiquity of consciousness, some argue that there is a distinction between sentience and consciousness. Since it is generally accepted that defining consciousness is problematic, perhaps looking at the idea of *sentience* will help. History of science professor Godfrey-Smith does that in his book *Other Minds*. He argues that "sentience" is "not a 'soul-like' substance that is somehow added

to the physical world as *dualists* think. Nor is it something which pervades nature as panpsychists believe." He argues:

> Sentience is brought into being *somehow* from the evolution of sensing and acting; it involves being a living system with a point of view on the world around it...Unless we conclude that all living things have a modicum of subjective experience—a view I don't regard as insane, but surely one that would need a lot of defense—there must be something about the way *animals* deal with the world that makes a crucial difference [my italics].[234]

Godfrey-Smith acknowledges that how sentience arose is a mystery, noting that it is brought into being "somehow" through the evolution of sensing and acting. But in so doing, he ignores the possibility that it may have been there from the beginning.

Theise and Kafatos attempt to define sentience as "sensing of the surrounding environment, complex processing of information that has been sensed (i.e., processing mechanisms defined by characteristics of a complex system), and generation of a response."[235] The authors argue that when complexity principles are carefully applied to an analysis of self-organization, from the largest to the smallest Planck scale of existence, at least some elements of consciousness appear wherever there is existence. They distinguish between the terms "consciousness" and "sentience," arguing that "sentience does not imply self-consciousness, which may be confined to higher species."[236] Self-consciousness implies sentience, but the authors argue that sentience can exist without self-consciousness. However, later in their paper, looking at the quantum realm, they acknowledge that due to the concepts of quantum entanglement and nonlocality, there is no "external" or "internal": "In the quantum realm one might tentatively suggest that the notion of 'sentience' be considered a simplest form of 'self-sentience,' i.e. nascent self-awareness."[237] If all this seems confusing, that's because it is: the terms "sentience" and "consciousness" are terms whose definitions are not universally agreed upon and that can be used to advance an agenda, which I will later show.

Brain as a Filter of Perception

As I mentioned, many scientists attempt to explain consciousness as something created by the brain. However, there is evidence that the primary function of the brain may be to filter out sensory information that is not essential for survival. The idea that the brain is a filtering mechanism has been suggested by such luminaries as C. D. Broad, Henri Bergson, and Aldous Huxley. Huxley suggested that "the function of the brain is in the main eliminative and not productive...The function of the brain and nervous system is to protect us from being overwhelmed [by sensory input]."[238]

This "filter theory" of the function of the brain has some intuitive appeal and may offer some validation of the reports of those who have had near-death experiences or who had unusual experiences under the influence of entheogens. Huxley described just such an experience when he was under the influence of mescaline. While in his garden, he observed that some red-hot pokers [flowers] "in full bloom, had exploded into my field of vision. So passionately alive that they seemed to be standing on the very brink of utterance, the flowers strained upwards into the blue."[239] Huxley's observation suggests that when the "reducing valve" is not doing its job (in this case due to the ingestion of hallucinogens), the possibility of plants being conscious at some level seems more plausible ("they seemed to be standing on the very brink of utterance").[240] When the brain's limiting power is completely suppressed, such as when a patient has had a heart attack and whose brain shows no activity, those who experience an NDE describe their clarity of thinking and competence as more enhanced than ever before, possibly due to the inactivity of the filter function of the brain.

The filter theory presents a novel way of looking at how the brain may facilitate altered states of consciousness (ASCs). For example, instead of the brain *causing* the ASC, it may, through impairment of the filter, allow the mind to experience something that is already present but imperceptible. This is an important distinction. Facco, Agrillo, and Greyson explain how

> sensations and feelings may enter consciousness only passing through the gate mediated by serotonin-2 and cannabinoid receptors, which behave like powerful *filters*. If so, the most energetic mental organs, including the gatekeeper to consciousness (serontonin-2), are likely to be the first to lose function in critical conditions (physical or existential), allowing for an enhancement of consciousness and emergence of NDEs and other NOMEs [nonordinary mental expressions], with their inescapable meaning [my italics].[241]

If we think of the brain "as eliminative and not productive," many of the anomalies discovered in the search for an understanding of how the brain and consciousness interact are explained: the brain is the gatekeeper to what the conscious mind perceives. There is evidence that trying to attribute "productive" qualities to the brain is problematic. One example of such a problem is evident from the work of John Lorber, a British neurologist at Sheffield University, who reports on an interesting case:

> There is a young student at this university who has an IQ of 126, has gained a first-class honors degree in mathematics and is socially completely normal. And yet the boy has virtually no brain...When we did a brain scan on him, we saw that instead of the normal 4.5-centimeter thickness of brain tissue between the ventricles and the cortical surface, there was just a thin layer of mantle measuring a millimeter or so. His cranium is filled mainly with cerebrospinal fluid.[242]

While this may seem like an exceptional case, there are others, such as that reported by Lionel Feuillet, a neurologist at the Mediterranean University in Marseille, France. Feuillet reported that a forty-four-year-old man who had a fluid-filled chamber that took up most of the room in his skull, and that left little more than a thin sheet of actual brain tissue, had an IQ of 75, was married, had two children, and worked as a civil servant.[243] Both the Lorber and Feuillet cases contribute to the weakening of the paradigm that holds that the brain is responsible for either consciousness or possibly even intelligence.

Sheldrake's morphogenetic field theory postulates that consciousness is "field-like." The brain may be just an organ that "transmits" consciousness but does not create or produce it. If one thinks of the brain like this, it explains everything from the mystery of mental powers where there is almost no brain, as well as the situation in which there is a delay in the decision to do something and the appearance of that in a brain wave. It is also in conformity with the idea that the brain acts as a filter of perceptions.

Consciousness at the Subatomic Level

Earlier, I stated that Heisenberg and others considered that consciousness may exist in the most simple of organisms. Does that imply that an electron or photon is conscious? Surprisingly, the answer may be yes. At the quantum level, "with quantum entanglement and non-locality operational for all possible units of existence (whether they are confirmed as multidimensional strings or some other structure), sentience is, in fact, universal."[244] While Theise and Kafatos have argued that sentience does not imply self-consciousness, it may imply a nascent form of self-awareness.

To better understand how this might be possible, consider the double-slit experiment in quantum physics. Richard Feynman, whom I quoted earlier, claimed that the double-slit experiment resulted in "a phenomenon which is impossible, *absolutely* impossible to explain in any classical way, and which has in it the heart of quantum mechanics. In reality, it contains the *only* mystery…the basic peculiarities of all quantum mechanics."[245]

The double-slit experiment confirmed the wave-particle duality of subatomic particles. What is the mystery that Feynman saw as impossible to explain in classical physics? It is the demonstrated fact that when light is shown on two slits, it passes through both slits as a wave. However, when photons, the subatomic components of light, are fired at the slits one at a time, they mysteriously "not only know whether or not both holes are open, they know whether or not we are watching them, and they adjust their behavior accordingly."[246]

Can one conclude from the fact that they "adjust their behavior accordingly" that the photons are conscious?

Clearly the subatomic particle does not have a brain or a nervous system, two requirements for consciousness required under materialist physics and biological paradigms. In fact Heisenberg made the following statement in his speech accepting the Nobel Prize in physics: "[The atom] has no immediate and direct physical properties at all." If the atom has no physical properties at all, and if we and everything else in the universe are comprised of atoms, a whole host of philosophical questions arises.[247]

Considering Heisenberg's statement and Bohm's argument for an interconnected reality, the question of the consciousness of the subatomic particle (in fact all particles, micro and macro) may be moot: there may be but one consciousness, and everything in the universe participates in it to a greater or lesser degree (Kastrup's argument in this chapter supports the idea that we are all part of one universal mind).

Herbert Spencer Jennings was a geneticist, zoologist, and eugenicist. He was educated at Harvard and spent much of his career at Johns Hopkins University. His books were, and still are, widely quoted in the fields of education, sociology, anthropology, and psychology.[248] In his book *Behavior of the Lower Organisms*, noting that humans were reluctant to attribute any qualities of mind to the lower organisms, he stated:

> The writer is thoroughly convinced, after long study of the behavior of this organism [protozoa], that if Amoeba were a large animal, so as to come within the everyday experience of human beings, its behavior would at once call forth the attribution to it of

states of pleasure and pain, of hunger, desire, and the like, on precisely the same basis as we attribute these things to the dog.[249]

As Jennings seems to be attributing what are generally considered "human traits" such as pleasure, pain, hunger, and desire to the lowly amoeba, what conclusions may we reach about those same traits exhibited in larger animals?

Christof Koch, a neuroscientist who had worked with Nobel Laureate Francis Crick, met with the Dalai Lama to discuss consciousness. Although they approached the topic differently, they were in agreement: consciousness is universal. They agreed that "any object with a phi greater than zero has consciousness. That would mean animals, plants,[250] cells, bacteria, and maybe even protons are conscious beings."[251] "Phi" is the Greek symbol used to denote whether a system is conscious, to what degree it is conscious, and what experiences that system is having.[252]

Are Animals Conscious?

Professors Trewavas and Baluska also argue that "consciousness in its many forms could well be ubiquitous, even down to the simplest of organisms."[253] They cite a 1902 presentation to the American Association for the Advancement of Science by Charles Minot:

A frank unbiased study of consciousness must convince every biologist that it is one of the fundamental phenomena of at least all animal life… Consciousness is a device to regulate the actions of organisms to accomplish purposes which are useful to organisms and are thus teleological [exhibit elements of design].

The terms *consciousness, sentience,* and *intelligence* are often used—or, in some cases, misused—interchangeably. It is imperative to recognize the moral implications of the meanings of those terms when attempting to define them as they relate to life that is nonhuman. I stated at the beginning of this chapter that many scientists (and even some philosophers!) consider it impossible to properly define consciousness. Nonetheless, if Kauffman is right in his assertion that no one really knows what consciousness is or how to properly define it, then why is the question of animal consciousness, much less the plant consciousness discussed below, so strenuously objected to? If the brain is not responsible for consciousness (or perhaps even intelligence), and if every *thing* is interconnected, is there any evidence that consciousness exists in not only human beings and other mammals, but in fish and even plants? One theory is that the thing that connects all living things is universal consciousness. If that is true, then all living things participate in this universal consciousness; the only difference is the degree to which that participation manifests in each living thing.

There are numerous studies which have concluded that fish feel pain and suffer much like birds and mammals. L. U. Sneddon, director of Bioveterinary Science at the University of Liverpool, was instrumental in discovering nociceptors that detect painful stimuli in fish. Sneddon has since published empirical studies that drive the fish welfare agenda in many contexts. Other researchers, notably Braithwaite in her book *Do Fish Feel Pain*, notes that although fish don't have brain structures strictly analogous to that of humans, "we have to look at behaviour and physiology," not just anatomy.[254] Needless to say, the idea that fish feel pain will not be easily accepted by many, who prefer to think of humans as unique examples of consciousness and self-reflection.

Speciesism is a form of discrimination based upon species membership.[255] In taking a position on consciousness in nonhuman species, one has to be careful that their views are not skewed by an attempt to exclude a species just because it isn't human. Inevitably this brings a moral dimension to the question, which lies far outside the materialist paradigm. Research on the question of animal consciousness shows how those who argue against the idea attempt to finesse their position by making a distinction that is not based upon fact, but rather upon furtherance of an agenda.

An example of the cruelty that can result from speciesism can be found in Thailand, where pig-tailed macaques are trained to pick coconuts for up to nine hours a day, six days a week. They are forced to wear a collar and are controlled by a tether tied to their handlers or wooden posts. When all the coconuts have been pulled from the tree, the chain is pulled, and the monkey comes down from the tree and scales the next tree. These monkeys are often worked to the point where they faint from exhaustion. This practice has been ongoing in Thailand for over four hundred years. It is only now that concerned individuals and organizations recognize this as animal cruelty and have begun to boycott coconuts picked by monkey labor. Speciesism facilitates this regrettable practice.

A metaphor drawing from Homer's classic tale *The Odyssey* illustrates how we might imagine our feelings for "persons" may be separated from our feelings for the "person" as represented by the human body. In the story, the witch Circe turns Odysseus's men into pigs:

They were like pigs-head, hair and all, and they grunted just as pigs do; but their senses were the same as before, and they remembered everything... Eurylochus hurried back to tell me about the sad fate of our comrades. He was so overcome with dismay that though he tried to speak he could find no words to do so; his eyes filled with tears and he could only sob and sigh, till at last we forced his story out of him, and he told us what had happened to the others.[256]

Eurylochus undeniably feels pity for the pigs that had been his shipmates, even though they were no longer in human form. The pity Eurylochus felt was no different than what he would have felt had the men been in human form. The importance here is that because he could tell that they retained memory of their human form, he knew what they were thinking. With animals we don't always know what they are thinking.

Philosophy professor David Cockburn wrote a paper, "Human Beings and Giant Squids," in which he recounts his reaction to seeing a nature program in which a giant squid was under threat from some other creature. He interpreted the squid's reaction to one of fear. In discussing two very different ways in which philosophers have attempted to address this display of emotion by a nonhuman animal, he notes:

My conviction that this is a being [say a giant squid or a fly] that is capable of suffering is to be grounded in the similarity between its body and behaviour and my body and behaviour; or between its body and behaviour and the bodies and behaviour of human beings in general. To the extent that this is so we have, surely, no choice but to concede that the weaker the similarities the weaker the conviction that is in place. While this has obvious implications for my thought about members of other races my immediate concern is with its implications for our thought about non-human species. If my conviction that other species feel pain or fear is to be grounded in their similarities to human beings then we must, it seems, concede that my conviction that dogs feel pain stands on much shakier ground than does my conviction that other human beings do; and my conviction that that giant squid was afraid may begin to look decidedly fragile...It may, at any rate, be very difficult to avoid the conclusion that our attempts to relieve the suffering of others should be concentrated on those about whom we can be most certain that they do suffer: those who look and behave most like us.[257]

He is arguing that the weaker the similarities in bodies to his and other human and nonhuman beings, the weaker the ability to discern suffering. I understand the point Cockburn is trying to make, but I take issue with his attempt to make a distinction between pain and suffering in humans and nonhuman beings. Why, for instance, does a nonhuman living thing, be it amoeba, dog, ape, or plant, respond to certain stimuli the way it does? How does seeing an animal react to pain cause us to feel? I suggest that we know when we see an animal act as we would if we were in pain, then we can conclude that the animal is in pain. This shared pain is evidence of what physics describes as "interconnectedness." Cockburn's thesis could be used by those who advocate not only for racism, but also speciesism, and carries with it the potential for acting without empathy for dissimilar living things.

Ann Long wrote a paper critical of Cockburn's thesis. [258] She quibbles with the difference between the words "pain" and "suffering," arguing that "pain and suffering are surely very different."[259] Quoting Brecht, she refers to Galileo, who avoided the pain of torture "by recanting what he knew to be true only to experience instead the suffering which is self-contempt." She goes on to insist that it is inappropriate and misleading to blur the distinction between pain and suffering. She sees suffering as a "self" phenomenon reserved especially for humans, with the possible exception of the higher apes, "where self-consciousness seems to begin to glimmer." In other words, she is arguing that an animal might feel pain, but it does not suffer; on its face, this idea strikes me as absurd. Many philosophers and psychologists consider the ability to transcend the Self as a path to experience the divine; to Long, however, the creature that she thinks has no sense of Self is to be looked upon as inferior to humans. [260] To support her argument, she cites a description by Jane Goodall in which a mother chimp died and her child seemed to grieve: "He avoided social contact, stopped eating, sat hunched and rocking for many hours a day...Within a week he too was dead." She notes that such reaction failed to trigger any show of consolation by other chimps: "No chimp has ever been reported to have consoled another." She draws from this that because a chimp can't see another chimp's woe, it has "no self-consciousness, therefore, no 'other' or 'thou' consciousness, therefore no recognition of, because no experience of, 'suffering.'" This attempt to draw a strong distinction between pain and suffering is another step toward speciesism. Long makes her position quite clear:

> The answer to the question "can I see another's woe, and not be in sorrow too?" would seem to be "no" for humans, but "yes" for chimps. And the reason? Perhaps because for chimps the "I" of "can I see?" is inappropriate. With no "I" there is no self-consciousness, therefore no "other" or "thou" consciousness, therefore no recognition of, because no experience of, "suffering."[261]

Long's claim that chimps do not console other chimps seems to be an attempt to make a distinction irrelevant to the question of suffering. Furthermore, Long's statement that "no chimp has ever been reported to have consoled another" is untrue. Research by primatologist and ethologist professor Franz de Waal has found the following:

> Expressions of empathy are common in apes and resemble those of our own species. In child research, for example, a family member is typically instructed to feign distress or pain, upon which touching, stroking, and close-up eye-contact by the child is interpreted as a sign of sympathetic concern. In chimpanzees, bystanders at a fight go over to the loser and put an arm around his or her shoulders or provide other calming contact.[262]

Long's argument, though false, has been used by those who would mistreat animals for their own ends—such as the exploitation of the macaques in Thailand.

In contrast to Long's argument against self-consciousness of all but humans, Trewavas and Baluska considered whether ants and bees were self-aware and noted that

> ants do not attack other nest mates but will attack
> other nests of the same species. Bees will attack hive
> intruders including other genotypes and recruit oth-
> ers to the attack by means of pheromones. All of this
> demonstrates perception and awareness of Self.[263]

Huxley offered an appropriate quote by Boethius on the knowledge of Self: "In other living creatures ignorance of self is nature; in man it is vice."[264] One might even argue that animals are "more conscious" than humans by looking at what Schopenhauer says about will-less knowledge: "[It] is reached by the consciousness of other things being raised to so high a potential that the consciousness of our selves vanishes."[265] Here the dissolution of our Self suggests a raising of consciousness. Schopenhauer again states: "In this way, all difference of individuality disappears so completely that it is all the same whether the perceiving eye belongs to a mighty monarch or a stricken beggar." Or perhaps even an animal? If animal consciousness becomes widely accepted, it will certainly lead to ethical and moral questions that threaten our way of looking at reality.

One unexpected source of support for the idea that animals are both intelligent and conscious comes from that pioneer of evolutionary theory Charles Darwin himself. His last book, *The Formation of Vegetable Mould Through the Action of Worms with Observations on Their*

Habits, was published in 1881. In that book, the author of that earlier work that is often cited in support of the argument against intelligent design, stated of the lowly earthworm that

> [i]f worms have the power of acquiring some notion, however rude, of the shape of an object and of their burrows, as seems to be the case, they deserve to be called intelligent; for they then act in nearly the same manner as would a man under similar circumstances.[266]

Surely if the great man of evolutionary theory can recognize intelligence in the earthworm, then there should be no great cry against the idea that other forms of animal life (and perhaps even plant life, as I will show) display not only intelligence, but potentially pain and suffering as well.

Marc Bekoff, professor emeritus of ecology and evolutionary biology at the University of Colorado, notes that skepticism as to the existence of emotions and morality in all but the human species has "dramatically dropped."[267] Bekoff argues that "dogs are full of natural goodness and have rich emotional lives." He notes that many animals can distinguish right from wrong. Looking at brain structures in dogs, he concludes, "Dogs apparently laugh. The same brain structures show the same activity in laughing humans and in dogs...A dog's laugh is a rhythmic pant." He also notes the following about dogs:

- They have a sense of fair play.

- They get jealous when a rival gets more or better treats or treatment.

- They are resentful, unnerved, or saddened by unfair behavior.

- They are made anxious by suspense.

- They get afraid.

- They are embarrassed when they mess up or do something clumsy.

- They feel remorse or regret when they do something wrong.

- They seek justice.

- They remember the bad things done to them but sometimes choose to forgive.

- They have affection and compassion for their animal and human friends and family.

- They defend loved ones.

- They grieve their losses.

- They have hope.

Bekoff cites Alfred North Whitehead, the English mathematician and philosopher, as having stated that the key elements of religious expression such as ritual and emotion are common to both humans and animals, but belief and rationalization are the exclusive province of humans. Bekoff disagrees, arguing that dogs think; they seek results that they want; they solve problems; and they have expectations and hopes. He concludes with the idea that if we have souls, then our animals have souls, and if we cannot know this for a fact, we should give them the benefit of the doubt. This is a major difference between the Christian religion and Buddhism. Saint Paul, citing Moses, seems to imply that God cares not for oxen. Although Pope Paul acknowledged that animals have souls in 1990, not all theologians would agree—some would argue that if animals do have souls, they are not immortal, as are the souls of humans. Buddhism, however, is clear on the point: "Buddhism teaches that all sentient beings are inseparably parts of a Whole, and that, consequently, there can be no true blissfulness for any until all attain the Other Shore."[268]

Do dogs, in particular, have unexplained powers that are manifestations of the ultimate reality? In Sheldrake's *Dogs That Know When Their Owners Are Coming Home*, just such a possibility is discussed. In his prefatory remarks concerning the lack of research into the unexplained power of animals, Sheldrake notes "the strength of the taboos against such inquiries."[269] He discusses three major classes of unexplained perceptiveness by animals: telepathy, sense of direction, and premonitions. He notes that invisible emotional bonds between people and animals are "a kind of hybrid between the bonds that animals form with each other and those that people form with each other." Sheldrake further proposes that such bonds are not metaphorical—they are literal connections, real in every way.[270] The idea of this real bond between animals extends to interspecies social bonds, such as that between pets and their owners. This idea of a "real" connection is consistent with the idea of entanglement at the quantum level, which I discussed previously. Sheldrake's book covers in detail the three classes of unexplained powers of animals, so I will not repeat all of that here. However, there is one unexplained power of animals that is particularly relevant to the topics discussed in this book: the unexplained ability of animals to respond to a distant situation of distress or death of an owner. Sheldrake has accumulated 177 accounts of dogs reacting to a death or accident of a human with whom the dog had a close relationship, and 62 accounts of cats doing likewise. One such case from 1968 is presented:

> My husband and I were on holiday in County Cork in Eire in April 1968, and on Easter Saturday my husband died very suddenly. Our seven-year-old Standard Poodle was staying with friends in St. Albans. At just after midnight the poodle howled and rushed upstairs to my friend, who was in the bath. At just after midnight my husband died.[271]

This case is typical of those reported by Sheldrake and certainly suggests a "real" connection between pets and their owners. Additionally, his database also includes thirty-two reports of humans knowing when their pet was in distress or had died at a distant location.[272] Most of these cases occurred when the people were awake, but interestingly some occurred in dreams.

Pets, and in particular dogs, seem to exhibit a kind of extrasensory perception. M. M. Moncrieff suggests this in *The Clairvoyant Theory of Perception*:

> All living things possess the faculties of Telepathy and Clairvoyance in various degrees…these E.S.P. faculties are important factors in all animal life… as animals…came to possess more developed mental powers with correspondingly more complicated

nervous systems…their clairvoyant and telepathic
powers decreased.

The most interesting observation by Moncrieff is his acknowledgment that "if a man possessed these faculties to any considerable
extent he would be so overwhelmed by the wealth of his telepathic
and clairvoyant impressions that he would be unable to function ef-
ficiently in his social and physical environment."[273] Compare this observation with Huxley's "reducing valve" metaphor discussed earlier.

Moncrieff goes further to explain his ideas about ESP and
animals, by reference to the activities of termites. Termites build
elaborate nests called termitaries. A large termitary may contain a
population of five hundred thousand individuals. Termites have very
primitive brains, which are little more than ganglia, and they are also
deaf and blind. How, one wonders, could such a large population
coordinate and work together to maintain the termitary? Today, the
explanation is given that the queen controls the workers and soldiers
by "pheromones." Moncrieff, referencing the work of Eugène Marais,
shows that it must be ESP, not pheromones, that coordinates and
organizes the termitary. Marais, in his book *Soul of the White Ant*,
originally published in 1937 before pheromones were discovered,
constructed a test to attempt to understand how the queen could
control her subjects. His test shows that the pheromone theory does
not explain the behavior of termites. He separated the queen of the
termitary from the rest of the termites by placing a steel plate several
feet into the ground. The workers on both sides of the steel plate
carried on their work as if there had been no change. Clearly this
shows that it is not pheromones that were being used by the queen to
control the workers and soldiers. If he killed the queen, all work on
both sides of the steel plate immediately stopped. Marais concluded

"the influence which streams from the queen is something intangible and similar to influence-at-a-distance which directs so many functions in highly developed animals."[274]

If the brain is not responsible for consciousness (or perhaps even intelligence or memory), and if every *thing* is interconnected (as quantum theory requires), is there any evidence that consciousness exists in not only human beings and other animals, but also in plants? An even more controversial idea is that plants can remember and can feel pain; the evidence that something important is going on in the plant world warrants consideration.

Are Plants Conscious?

There is robust scientific evidence that plants do have a capability of memory. Stefano Mancuso, a professor of plant science at the University of Firenze, and Monica Gagliano, a research associate in evolutionary ecology at the University of Western Australia, have devised an experiment to determine whether plants could learn to distinguish between harmless and harmful stimuli, and to remember that information. The plants were able to remember which stimulus was which and react accordingly for more than forty days—"a very long time if compared to the standard memory span of many insects and closer to the standard of several superior animals."[275] It's even more amazing when one realizes that plants have no brains. Perhaps Sheldrake's theory of morphic fields can help to explain how plants remember.

Are plants conscious? An even more contentious idea is that plants can feel pain. The idea that plants are conscious and feel pain deserves serious consideration, in light of recent research. It is much easier to accept the idea that dogs are conscious than it is to believe plants are conscious. How could one go about finding out if plants are conscious? If we apply the same tests to plants that we apply to nonhuman vertebrates, we find the results confounding: our confidence that plants are not conscious is called into question.

One of the most persuasive examples of the extraordinary abilities of plants can be seen in a time-lapse video prepared by Mancuso. The video shows a bean plant growing in the professor's laboratory. Approximately four feet away is a support pole. The bean plant is waving in the air as if to ascertain where the support is. While it is waving back and forth, it is forming a sort of hook at its end, which eventually is used to latch on to the pole. How does the plant even know there is a support pole there? Surely it cannot see as animals see, so there is something else going on. Somehow it knows (senses?) there is a support nearby, and it is attempting to reach it. It is difficult not to see that the plant has intelligence and purpose in its actions, much as one would ascribe to animals, including humans.[276]

Gagliano has come to this conclusion: "[T]he process of remembering may not require the conventional neural networks and pathways of animals; brains and neurons are just one possible, undeniably sophisticated, solution, but they may not be a necessary requirement for learning."[277] Gagliano also studied plants to determine whether they exhibited any traits that might indicate "intelligence." In particular, she looked to see if plants could learn from their environment. Using the same theory and analytical methods found in animal-learning research, she found that plants demonstrate long-lasting, learned behavior, which matches that found in animals. If we do not feel empathy when a plant acts a certain way, perhaps it is because we haven't looked closely at how it is responding to predators or threats.

An early (1876) serious look at plants' intelligence was done by Dr. W. Lauder Lindsay, an MD. His paper "Mind in Plants" was published in *The British Journal of Psychiatry*. In that paper, he discusses the problems he faced trying to do work in a paradigm challenging field such as plant intelligence:

> Moreover, some Botanists are influenced, apparently, by that most contemptible form of ignorance and bigotry which refuses to believe, or even to examine, facts, or to accept words, names, or phrases that seem to militate against their baseless religious preconceptions and misconceptions.[278]

In his paper, Lindsay identified nineteen characteristics of a mind, which plants share with animals. The most startling conclusion Lindsay reached in his work with plants was this:

> I hold, on the contrary, that unless we re-define the term *consciousness*, we must regard some form or degree of it as occurring in both *animals and plants that are destitute not only of brain, but of a nervous system.*[279]

This shows that even in the early work with plants, before the discoveries of quantum mechanics, there were anomalies noted in the way plants behaved when subjected to certain stimuli. These anomalies raised questions as to whether or not a nonanimal species demonstrated an awareness to its environment, much like animals (including humans) do.

William James, the founder of American psychology, delivered a series of lectures at Manchester College. Lecture IV was titled "Concerning Fechner." Fechner was a physicist and philosopher and was highly esteemed by James. In that lecture, he complimented Fechner, stating that "[he] had vision and that is why one can read him over and over again, and each time bring away a fresh sense of reality." What is relevant to the discussion here is Fechner's view on the consciousness of plants. He acknowledged that because plants have no central nervous system, they can have no consciousness (as it was thought of at the time). But he argues that the consciousness of plants may be of a different type:

> With nothing to do but to drink the light and air with their leaves, to let their cells proliferate, to feel their rootlets draw the sap, is it conceivable that they should not consciously suffer if water, light, and air are suddenly withdrawn? Or that when the flowering and fertilization which are the culmination of their life take place, they should not feel their own existence more intensely and enjoy something like we call pleasure in ourselves?[280]

Jack Schultz, a Dartmouth College biologist, is hesitant to say that trees have consciousness or an awareness of their environment. He does say, however, that "[t]rees can do amazing things, and we're just beginning to find out how complicated their behavior is. They're like very slow animals—the only thing they can't do is run away."[281]

Researchers Peter Tompkins and Christopher Bird wrote a book in which they chronicled the reaction of plants to their surroundings.[282] They came to believe that plants are more than just roots and branches; they exhibit intelligence, memory, and emotion.[283] One reviewer of their book, Richard Klein, professor of Botany at the University of Vermont, made the following comment on their work:

> If I can't "get inside a plant" or "feel emanations"
> from a plant and don't know anyone else who can,
> that doesn't detract one whit from the possibility
> that some people can and do…According to *The
> Secret Life of Plants*, plants and men do interrelate,
> with plants exhibiting empathetic and spiritual rela-
> tionships and showing reactions interpreted as dem-
> onstrating physical-force connections with men. As
> my students say, "hey, wow!"[284]

As one would expect, the work of Tompkins and Bird has not escaped criticism—primarily due to the inability of some to recreate the experiments mentioned in the book. However, as I have previously mentioned, quantum physics tells us that the observer creates reality with their measurements. If the scientists who attempted to recreate the experiments discussed in the book were unable to achieve the same results, was it due to their bias against the ideas being tested? Surprisingly, the answer may be "yes." The anomaly is discussed by Richard Milton, who references the work of Kuhn, whom I discussed earlier:

> The idea is one that many people, including scien-
> tists, will find impossible to accept. Are we really
> being asked to believe that when scientist "A" looks
> at an experimental result he sees one thing, but when
> scientist "B" looks at the same experiment he sees
> something quite different, because of differences
> in their personality? Extraordinary though it may
> sound, that is exactly the conclusion that Kuhn
> and others have reached. And the evidence from

the history of science is not merely persuasive, it is overwhelming.[285]

Cleve Backster, a CIA polygraph expert, hooked up a polygraph to plants, specifically a dracaena he had in his office. Backster observed patterns on the graph when a leaf was torn off or if he simply imagined setting fire to the plant, which were similar to what would be seen if a human were feeling stress. The scientific community discredited the work when experimenters failed to duplicate his findings. This failure to duplicate Backster's results may be due to the failure of the experimenter and the plant to establish an emotional connection—perhaps not altogether different from the participation required of an observer to collapse the wave function discussed earlier.[286]

Whether or not plants have minds or consciousness is not even considered a serious question by some scientists, who scoff at the idea that consciousness, whatever it is, can be a property of anything other than a human being. This is due, in part, to the lack of agreement among scientists and psychologists as to what a "mind" is, or what "consciousness" is (or a failure to consider that their bias may be an example of the "speciesism" discussed previously).

Is the brain the storehouse of memory? Claiming that memories are physically stored in the brain is problematic. Wilder Penfield, an American-Canadian neurosurgeon, stimulated the temporal lobes of the brains of individuals suffering from epilepsy with electrical probes. He found that he could elicit vivid memories from these patients, who interpreted these memories as things that they had done previously. However, based upon a lifetime of studying the brain, Penfield concluded in his last book *The Mystery of the Mind* that memory was not stored in the brain.[287] Some cells in the brain die and are replaced by new ones all the time. If the brain is the storehouse of memories, how is it that we feel like the same person as we go through time?[288]

There are two arguments concerning the location of memory that are worthy of consideration. The first is the "systemic memory hypothesis," which argues that living cells possess memory. The second is the idea that memory is stored in a nonlocal field.

Systemic Memory Hypothesis

Systemic memory hypothesis (SMH) is a theory that is based upon the idea that since recurrent feedback loops exist in all atomic, molecular, and cellular systems, there should be evidence of memory in those systems. One of the predictions of SMH allows for the possibility that "sensitive recipients of transplanted organs can experience aspects of the donor's personal history stored in the transplanted tissues." While at first this sounds inconceivable, there is evidence that it may be true.

Pearsall, Schwartz, and Russek wrote a paper titled "Changes in Heart Transplant Recipients that Parallel the Personalities of their Donors."[289] The paper reported ten cases in which the personality of the recipient changed after the transplant procedure to exhibit traits of the donor. Selected cases exhibiting those changes, which were confirmed by the donors' and recipients' families or friends, are presented below.

Case 1. The donor was an eighteen-year-old boy killed in a car crash. The donor's father, a psychiatrist, stated that his son "always wrote poetry" and was a practicing musician. The recipient was an eighteen-year-old girl with endocarditis and heart failure. The recipient's father reported that his daughter had been "a hell-raiser" until she got sick. After the transplant, she said she felt the desire to play an instrument and sing. The first song she composed was about her new heart as being her lover's heart.

Case 2. The donor was a sixteen-month-old boy who had drowned in a bathtub. The donor's mother, a physician, stated that she could more than hear her son's heart—she could feel it within her. She visited the recipient's family when her son's heart was five years old, beating in the now six-year-old recipient. The recipient had the same baby-talk words and played with the donor's mother's nose, just as her son had. She notes that she is a doctor who was trained to be a keen observer and was always a skeptic. She feels that "on some level, our son is still alive." Her feelings about the recipient's actions mirroring those of her son's were confirmed by the recipient's parents. The donor had mild cerebral palsy on his left side. The recipient now has stiffness and shaking on his left side, which he never exhibited prior to the transplant.

Case 3. The donor was a seventeen-year-old African American male student, who was killed in a drive-by shooting on his way to a violin lesson. The donor loved classical music; he died holding on to his violin case. The recipient was a forty-seven-year-old Caucasian laborer. The recipient claims that after the transplant he developed a love for classical music, which he hated before the transplant. He stated that "I used to hate classical music, but now I love it…I more than like it. I play it all the time." He knew that his heart had come from an African American and presumed that the donor would have preferred rap music.

Case 4. The donor was a nineteen-year-old woman killed in a car crash. She was into health food, operating her own health-food store. She would scold her mother about not being a vegetarian. Her mother said her daughter was into free love and had a different man in her life every few months. As she was dying, she told her mother over and over again that she could feel the impact of the car hitting her. The recipient was a twenty-nine-year-old woman. After the transplanted heart, she noted that she could feel the impact in her chest of the accident the donor experienced. She also stated that after the transplant, she hated meat, whereas before the transplant, she was "McDonald's biggest moneymaker, and now meat makes me throw up. Actually, when I even smell it, my heart starts to race." Most significantly, the recipient became engaged to a "great guy and we love each other. The sex is terrific." Before the transplant she was gay. She jokingly suggests she "got a gender transplant."

All the above cases challenge our notion that the brain is the storehouse of memory. Pearsall notes in this paper that "in addition to heart recipients, kidney, liver, and other organ recipients also indicated changes in sense of smell, food preference, and emotional factors." The authors posit that "cellular memory, possibly systemic memory, is a plausible explanation for these parallels." I suggest that such cellular memory might be thought of as an "imprint" into the cells by the donor, and not necessarily the location of the memory which would be available to the donor when he or she was alive. Whatever the explanation, clearly more research is necessary to better understand the phenomenon. The University of Arizona is conducting research on more than three hundred transplant cases to determine the frequency of such phenomena.

Field Theories of Memory

Quantum theory is predicated on the assumption that physical reality is immaterial; fields are the only reality. It is not matter that makes up the universe, it is fields.[290] This principle of quantum physics supports the notion that memories are stored in fields rather than in the brain itself. There are many different names for such fields, each with their own special attributes. I prefer to think of the differently named field theories as descriptive of one field with many attributes. Whether it is called the akashic field, or the morphic field, or some other name, the idea that a field is the substance of the universe is compatible with the idea that there is an ultimate reality, behind the doors of perception, which embodies these fields and from which they emanate.

Sheldrake, whom I discussed in Chapter 2 and earlier in this chapter, has revolutionary ideas about memory. Sheldrake argues that memory is stored in a "morphic field," as opposed to a brain. He suggests our brains are more like computer terminals that can access the "cloud," which stores all memory since the beginning of time. As one would expect, his ideas are roundly rejected by mainstream science. In trying to explain how fields account for memory, Sheldrake uses the example of brain damage that results in a loss of memory. The conventional view is that loss of memory from brain damage results from the destruction of memory traces, a destruction of the ability to recall those memories, or both. The fact that after the loss of abilities, patients often recover "partially or completely" even though the damaged brain tissues do not regenerate, can be explained by the morphic field theory.[291] The "morphic field" theory may support the idea of reincarnation discussed in Chapter 7. Morphic field theory might also contribute to the discussion on synchronicity discussed in Chapter 3.

Morphic fields may also help to understand how learning is transferred across great distances. Lyall Watson, an Australian botanist, relates the following:

> Off the coast of Japan are a number of tiny islands where the resident populations of macaques have

been under continuous observation for more than twenty years. The scientists provide supplementary food, but the monkeys also feed themselves by digging up sweet potatoes and eating them dirt and all. This uncomfortable practice continued unchanged for many years until one day a young male monkey broke with tradition and carried his potato down to the sea where he washed it before eating it. He taught the trick to his mother, who showed it to her current mate and so the culture spread through the colony until most of them, let us say 99 monkeys, were doing it. Then one Tuesday morning at eleven, the hundredth individual acquired the habit, and within an hour, it appeared on two other islands in two physically unconnected populations of monkeys who until that moment had shown no inclination to wash their food.[292]

Although this narrative is proffered as an example of Sheldrake's morphic field theory, it also relates to Jung's theory of synchronicity. Another example of the overlap between the theories of morphic fields and synchronicity might be the famous dispute between the polymath Gottfried Leibniz and Isaac Newton as to who invented calculus. Leibniz had published his work first but was accused of plagiarizing the unpublished work of Newton. The parallels to Watson's story of the macaques to the squabble between Newton and Leibniz are obvious.

Split Brains and Consciousness

Split-brain surgery has been performed as a method to enable those who suffer from severe cases of epilepsy to live a more normal life unplagued by seizures, convulsions, or falling. The surgery's technical reference is "corpus callosotomy." There have been attempts to use the results of experiments conducted on split-brain patients to better understand consciousness; however, some of the conclusions drawn from those experiments are problematic. One problem arises from the implications of what has been referred to as the "astonishing hypothesis" of Francis Crick, in which it is held that

> you, your joys and your sorrows, your memories and your ambitions, your sense of personal identity and free will, are in fact no more than the behavior of a vast assembly of nerve cells and their associated molecules...You're nothing but a pack of neurons.[293]

Crick was an "epiphenomenalist," or one who believes that consciousness is an epiphenomenon of neural processes of the brain, which I discussed previously. The question here is to determine whether split-brain patients can offer support for the astonishing hypothesis. I believe such patients do not provide such support.

Hoffman believes the astonishing hypothesis "offers a cogent explanation: if consciousness arises from the interactions of a pack of neurons, then splitting that pack—and their interactions—can split consciousness." He then asks, "What could it mean to split my feelings, my knowledge, my emotions, my beliefs, my personality, my very self?"[294] A statement Hoffman makes to support Crick's epiphenomenalist view—that just because you can't explain how neural activity causes conscious experiences, such as the color red, doesn't mean that there is no explanation—provides a slippery slope: "Our failure to envision a mechanism does not preclude one."[295] This is another application of the specious "absence of evidence is not evidence of absence" argument, which I described previously.

I am not sure whether Hoffman would refer to himself as an epiphenomenalist, but his arguments in support of those who advocate such a theory lead me suppose that he is. In support of his analysis of the evidence provided by split-brain surgery's effect on consciousness, he cites three papers from 1974, 1994, and 2006. He chooses to ignore a more recent paper from 2017, which argues that when the brain is split, it divides perception but not consciousness. The authors of that paper which was published by Oxford University Press conclude the following:

> Severing the cortical connections between two hemispheres does not seem to lead to two independent conscious agents within one brain...This raises the intriguing possibility that even without massive communication between cerebral hemispheres, and thus increased modularity, unity in consciousness and responding is largely preserved.[296]

Dissociative Identity Disorder (DID)

DID is a widely contested phenomenon within the field of psychology, but I am including a discussion of it because it may have explanatory power in trying to bridge universal interconnectedness or entanglement, a proven characteristic of the quantum world, with consciousness and the perception of Self. The definition of DID follows:

> A dissociative disorder characterized by the pres-
> ence of two or more (sometimes many) separate
> personalities, each with its own memories and pat-
> terns of behavior, at least two of which take turns in
> recurrently taking control of behavior, the disorder
> also being characterized by amnesia for personal
> information that is too great to be attributable to
> ordinary forgetfulness…the disorder is the subject
> of considerable controversy and is not universally
> recognized.[297]

The possible relevance of DIDs to ASCs follows from research done by Kastrup. He suggests that the individual personality is a "split-off" complex of the universal mind (which I have alluded to throughout this book). If one accepts the reality of DIDs, it follows that the relationship of consciousness to the body is more complex than what epiphenomenalism argues. Although the definition I have given includes the disclaimer that the condition of DID "is not uni-versally recognized," I will present two cases that I feel lend credence to the reality of the condition.

The first case involves a thirty-three-year-old patient who had been involved in an accident thirteen years earlier.[298] This is a fas-cinating case and provides some evidence of the validity of DID. The patient exhibited more than ten "alters" [personalities], which differed by age, gender, attitudes, temperament, and other factors, including voice and language. Some alters spoke only English, others only German. When arriving for therapy, she was always accompa-nied by her guide dog. Some of her alters were blind; others reported normal vision. Electroencephalogram (EEG) activity showed that the brain function expected with normal sight was not present when a blind alter was in control of the body. The expected brain activity recorded by the EEG was present when a sighted alter was in control of the body.

The second case involves a study reported in the *New York Times*, and discussed a woman who had three alters, aged five, seventeen, and thirty-five. The five-year-old alter had a condition known as "lazy eye," which appears as one eye turned toward the nose. This condition was not exhibited in either the seventeen or thirty-five-year-old alters.[299] The *Times* article noted that "there is a strong psychological separation between each sub-personality [alter]; each will have his own name and age, and often some specific memories and abilities. Frequently, for example, personalities will differ in handwriting, artistic talent or even in knowledge of foreign languages."

The phenomenon of DID complicates our understanding of the nature of consciousness, the Self, and the relationship between the mind and the body. What strikes me as particularly relevant are the documented physical changes in the body when there is a change in alters. This is an area in need of more research.

Kastrup has an interesting theory that the brain is *in* the mind, not the mind in the brain. He argues that dissociative identity disorder is evidence that each individual is a split-off complex of universal mind, or what I have called ultimate reality. He observes:

> [The] fragmentation of the human psyche into multiple and seemingly separate identities happens all the time...psychology informs us of countless cases of the phenomenon of "Dissociative Identity Disorder," in which a single person can display multiple and seemingly disconnected identities and personalities...I contend that each one of us

is a split-off complex of the one medium of mind underlying all existence.[300]

In Chapter 2, I presented Bohm's argument that quantum physics treats the entire realm of existence, hidden and manifest, as an unbroken, interconnected whole. If this is the case, perhaps it is not necessary to think of a subatomic particle as having consciousness, but rather that the subatomic particle and the observer who created the experiment are connected through one ubiquitous consciousness: a universal mind.[301]

Kastrup goes on to clarify what his theory means. Substance dualism—the idea that there exist both matter and an immortal soul—is closer to describing reality than is materialism. He argues that substance dualism predicts that consciousness does not end upon physical death and is also supportive of the idea of "an enduring 'personal consciousness' in the form of an invisible soul."[302] Credible evidence supporting Kastrup's theory as to the immortality of consciousness is presented in Chapter 7.

6

Altered States of Consciousness

To sleep—perchance to dream: ay, there's the rub.
—William Shakespeare, *Hamlet*

THERE IS A CERTAIN IRONY in attempting to define ASCs in light of Kaufmann's claim that "nobody has the faintest idea what consciousness is…I don't have any idea. Nor does anybody else, including the philosophers of mind." Even though we do not fully understand consciousness, we do know that an altered state of consciousness is significantly different from our "normal" waking consciousness.

Arnold Ludwig, an MD, has proposed the following definition:

> [ASCs are]…any mental state(s), induced by various physiological, psychological, or pharmacological maneuvers or agents, which can be recognized subjectively by the individual himself (or by an objective observer of the individual) as representing a sufficient deviation in subjective experience

or psychological functioning from certain general norms for that individual during alert, waking consciousness.[303]

"States of consciousness" refers to the entire range in which conscious experiences may be organized.[304] ASCs include

- gratuitous experiences of the sacred;

- religious experiences,[305], [306]

- meditation;

- dreams;

- experiences under the influence of entheogens;

- out-of-body experiences;

- near-death experiences; and

- hypnosis.

Gratuitous Experiences of the Sacred[307]

Ultimate reality is not only implied from evidence of its manifestation in perceptual reality in the manner discussed in Chapter 2, but it may also be experienced as the "feeling of the 'uncanny,' the thrill of awe of reverence, the sense of independence, of impotence, or of nothingness, or again, the feeling of religious rapture and exaltation."[308] These are experiences of the numinous and of the sacred. They are transpersonal in that they show the individual an ultimate reality beyond ordinary ego consciousness.

Emerson describes such an encounter with the numinous in his essay *Nature*:

> In the woods, we return to reason and faith. There I feel nothing can befall me in life—no disgrace, no calamity, (leaving my eyes), which nature cannot repair. Standing on the bare ground—my head bathed by the blithe air, and uplifted into space—all mean egotism vanishes. I become a transparent eyeball; I am nothing; I see all; the currents of the Universal Being circulate through me; I am part or particle of God.[309]

Another example of an encounter with the numinous is recounted by Garcia-Romeu and Tart. It was written in 1872 in the third person to convey a sense of objectivity:

> He was in a state of quiet, almost passive enjoyment. All at once, without warning of any kind, he found himself wrapped around as it were by a flame colored cloud. For an instant he thought of fire, some sudden conflagration in the great city, the next he knew that the light was within himself. Directly afterwards came upon him a sense of exultation, of immense joyousness, accompanied or immediately followed by an intellectual illumination quite impossible to describe. Into his brain streamed one momentary lightning flash of the Brahmic Splendor

> which has ever since lightened his life; upon his heart fell one drop of things he did not come to believe, he saw and knew that the Cosmos is not dead matter but a living Presence, that the soul of man is immortal, that the universe is so built and ordered that without any peradventure all things work together for the good of each and all, that the foundation principle of the world is what we call love and that the happiness of every one in the long run is absolutely certain.[310]

There are hundreds of such cases in the literature, but what remains a mystery is why or how such experiences occur spontaneously and unexpectedly. These experiences are those that Corbett referred to "as direct experiences of the sacred." They are not phenomena that arise in the brain, but rather perceptions that occur due to a failure of the brain's "reducing valve" function:

> Mind at large has to be funneled through the reducing valve of the brain and nervous system. What comes out the other end is a measly trickle of the kind of consciousness which will help us stay alive.[311]

Rudolf Otto and others have argued that direct experience of the sacred has formed the basis of all religion. Otto used the term *mysterium tremendum et fascinans* to describe an experience that is both tremendous and fascinating, something "uncanny, not of our ordinary world," something that is ineffable.[312] The experiences of ultimate reality provide more than just an implication as to its existence. Carl Jung relates such an experience after he slipped into unconsciousness after a heart attack. I consider his experience a "gratuitous experience of the sacred" rather than a near-death experience, due to its similarity to that described by Emerson:

> I found myself in an utterly transformed state. It was as if I were in an ecstasy…"This is eternal bliss," I thought. "This cannot be described; it is far too wonderful"…I can describe the experience only as the ecstasy of a non-temporal state in which past, present, and future are one…I was woven into an indescribable whole and yet observed it with complete objectivity.[313]

William James cites an example of an experience that he terms "mystical consciousness." In *The Varieties of Religious Experience*, he relates a description of the experience reported by the poet J. A. Symonds:

> Suddenly…at church or, in company, or when I was reading, and always, I think, when my muscles were at rest, I felt the approach of the mood. Irresistibly it took possession of my mind and will, lasted what seemed an eternity, and disappeared in a series of rapid sensations which resembled the awakening from anesthetic influence. One reason why I disliked this kind of trance was that I could not describe it to myself. I cannot even now find words to render it intelligible [this from a poet!]. It consisted in a gradual but swiftly progressive obliteration of space, time, sensation, and the multitudinous factors

of experience which seem to qualify what we are pleased to call our Self. In proportion as these conditions of ordinary consciousness were subtracted, the sense of an underlying or essential consciousness acquired intensity. At last nothing remained but a pure, absolute, abstract Self. The universe became without form and void of content. But Self persisted, formidable in its vivid keenness, feeling the most poignant doubt about reality...The return to ordinary conditions of sentient existence began by my first recovering the power of touch, and then by the gradual though rapid influx of familiar impressions and diurnal interests. At last I felt myself once more a human being; and though the riddle of what is meant by life remained unsolved, I was thankful for this return from the abyss—this deliverance from so awful an initiation into the mysteries of skepticism.[314]

The experience described by Symonds is another example of a gratuitous experience of the sacred. Two other such examples are given by James:[315]

I remember the night, and almost the very spot on the hilltop, where my soul opened out, as it were, into the Infinite, and there was a rushing together of the two worlds, the inner and the outer. It was a deep calling unto deep—the deep that my own struggle had opened up...I stood alone with Him who had made me, and all the beauty of the world, and love, and sorrow, and even temptation. I did not seek Him, but felt the perfect unison of my spirit with His...For the moment nothing but an ineffable joy and exaltation remained.

And:

I have on a number of occasions felt that I had enjoyed a period of intimate communion with the divine. These meetings came unasked and unexpected...What I felt on these occasions was a temporary loss of my own identity, accompanied by an illumination which revealed to me a deeper significance...It is in this that I find my justification for saying that I have enjoyed communication with God.

Religious Experiences

James defined religion as "the feelings, acts, and experiences of individual men in their solitude, so far as they apprehend themselves to stand in relation to whatever they may consider the divine."[316] Huston Smith's acclaimed work *The World's Religions* identifies seven major historical religions: Hinduism, Buddhism, Confucianism, Taoism, Islam, Judaism, and Christianity. Smith also recognizes primal religions, noting that while the historical religions cover a period of less than four thousand years, the primal religions have existed for three million years or so.[317] It is generally understood that those who considers themselves religious belong to, and practice according to, a religious tradition.[318] Prayer, the power of which has been discussed previously, is considered by Teasdale to be a communion with ultimate reality, regardless as to whether it is personal, impersonal (transpersonal), or beyond both. Teasdale argues "Everything is an avenue leading to the experience of Ultimate Reality," adding that "the divine communicates itself in all things." This is what I have argued throughout this book: the sacred ultimate reality is everywhere—we need only recognize it.[319]

Religious experiences differ somewhat from other kinds of experiences in altered states of consciousness. They are distinguishable from mystical experiences because although mystical experiences are religious, not all religious experiences can be considered mystical.[320]

Three religious figures in history who reported having had religious experiences are Saint Paul, Moses, and Muhammad. The religious experiences of the followers of the various religions differ, but there are certain elements of the experiences that are common to all religions. In order to explore those commonalities, guidelines were developed by Thomas Keating, an American Trappist monk, to facilitate interfaith discussion and identify those attributes that would further interfaith understanding.[321] The guidelines that he proposed include the following:

1. An acknowledgment of the place of ultimate reality in all the religions of the world.

2. Recognition that ultimate reality cannot be limited by any name or concept.

3. Our mystical process depends on our relationship or connection to the elusive mystery.

4. In order to actualize our innate potential for infinite life and development, we need to follow the path of faith.

5. We are all mystics by virtue of our birth. We are meant for something more. All the religions inform us of this truth, and their many forms of spirituality are ways for each one of us to nurture the awakening.

6. Everything is an avenue leading to the experience of ultimate reality. The divine communicates itself in all things.

Keating saw the importance of recognizing that all faiths share a desire to know and experience ultimate reality, a reality that expresses itself in all things if one just takes the time to look.

Meditation

Meditation can produce an altered state of consciousness that may provide access to ultimate reality. Huxley recognized this power of meditation:

> Meditation, in other words, is the technique of mysticism. Properly practiced, with due preparation, physical, mental and moral, meditation may result in a state of what has been called "transcendental consciousness"—the direct intuition of, and union with, an intimate spiritual reality [ultimate reality] that is perceived as simultaneously beyond the Self and in some way within it.[322]

Master Sheng-yen, a Chinese Buddhist monk, gave a description of the ecstatic state attainable through meditation. Note how it compares to the ecstatic state described by both Emerson and Jung:

> That feeling of unification with the universe is actually one kind of samadhi [meditative absorption], a result of a deep state of concentration, and when a person is at this stage, they recognize that the entire universe is the same as themselves...So at this point, one would no longer have individual selfish ideas or individual selfish thoughts that normally arise from the narrow, selfish ego. In fact, one may experience a tremendous power that would result from this samadhi, a power that would come from the idea that "the universe is the same as me."[323]

The behavioral descriptions of meditation refer to the following elements: relaxation, concentration, altered state of awareness, abeyance of rational thought, and concentration on the self. Historically, meditation was an element of religious practice. In psychotherapy, meditation taught patients to become aware of the problem before attempting to solve it, to practice forbearance, and "to come to terms with 'what is,' rather than fight hopelessly for 'what might be,' or 'might have been.'"[324]

Psi (psychic or paranormal phenomena) may be experienced during the initial stages of meditation as one becomes aware of deeper levels of reality.[325] One study of meditation and psychokinesis (PK) between 1971 and 1988 found that the majority of practitioners of meditation exhibited a stronger PK effect.[326]

Dreams

Our consciousness passes into the hidden realm when we dream. However, since our consciousness is not active, the dreams are often a random collection of scenes, people, and activities.

Mutual dreams are similar dreams of two or more individuals on the same night. Shared dreams are more specific than mutual dreams. Psychologist Stanley Krippner explains that in shared dreams, the dreamers (two or more) "claim to have met in the same time and space during the dream."[327] Shared dreams are also mentioned by Stanford researcher Stephen LaBerge, who finds support for the idea that in some ways the dream world may be just as real as the objective, physical world.[328] "This is because the primary criterion for 'objectivity' is that an experience is shared by more than one person—a fact supposedly true of both mutual and shared dreams."[329] LaBerge asks, "In that case, what would happen to the traditional dichotomy between dreams and reality?"[330] He goes on to say:

> A wealth of anecdotal evidence supports the idea that ESP [extrasensory perception] occurs, working across both space and time. If it is indeed possible to perceive, in some fashion, events happening at a distance, or even those that have not yet happened, space and time must be other than what they seem, and the same goes for subjective and objective realities![331]

Contrary to popular opinion, dreams are not restricted to only rapid eye movement (REM) sleep. Dreams occur in all the various stages of sleep and, like other ASCs, exhibit a virtual sense of reality and a greater sense of visual perceptions.[332] In many spontaneous dreams, the experience of self-reflection is inconsequential. While there may be some control in spontaneous dreams, that, too, is inconsequential.

Lucid dreaming, however, "is the experience of achieving conscious awareness of dreaming while still asleep."[333] A lucid dream generally occurs when a subject is asleep and experiencing REM. When our consciousness is active within the dream world, we are able to consciously construct our dream world out of all the possibilities. If duality is a fact of existence, after the death of the body, our consciousness may continue to exist in a "lucid dream world" limited only by our imagination.

The earliest report of a lucid dream in Western history is in a letter dated AD 415 by Saint Augustine. Augustine's letter mentions a physician who had doubted whether there was an afterlife. In a lucid dream, the physician was taken to a beautiful city where he heard singing "so exquisitely sweet as to surpass anything he had ever heard." After this dream the physician's doubts of an afterlife were completely dismissed.[334]

The physician's experience is reinforced by Physicist Fred Alan Wolf, who is quoted as saying, "Such dreams are actually visits to parallel realities."[335]

The parallel realities to which Wolf alludes represent the ultimate or divine reality that lies beyond the doors of perception. When the dreamer accesses this portal, they find the realm from which creativity originates. From that realm, creativity passes through the portal, finding its way into the world of perception and into a receptive mind.[336]

This sacred realm provides access to that which exists in the unconscious: "Most of our knowledge is unconscious—tacit, implicit, and difficult to verbalize. The very ground upon which consciousness stands is the unconscious mind."[337] Corbett goes further, arguing that the inspiration for creative acts does not arise from the personal Self. Those ideas that have been the inspiration for great works of art and discoveries in mathematics and science appear to come from nowhere; their source is a mystery even to the artist or scientist.[338]

The creativity that arises from this sacred realm is accessible through dreams.[339] Psychologist Ann Faraday reminds us that dreams may provide the inspiration for great works of art: the plot for *Dr. Jekyll and Mr. Hyde* was conceived in a dream, as was the invention of the sewing machine.[340] More recent examples of the dream source of well-known artistic compositions include Paul McCartney's "Yesterday." McCartney had a dream one night in his attic bedroom, awoke with a melody in his head that he could not ignore, and immediately went to his piano and played it. The tune had come to him in his dream almost complete. Although the words to the music were not provided along with the melody, he eventually crafted what would become "Yesterday," now the most recorded song ever. This beautiful song has been enjoyed by millions—and it came from a dream.[341]

One of the most impressive examples of the power of dreams to inspire creative thought is that of Srinivasa Ramanujan, an Indian mathematician who lived in India during the British Raj. Ramanujan was uneducated, having failed in his attempts at school. He taught himself mathematics and wrote volumes of theorems and equations, which are, even today, being recognized as far ahead of their time. There is some mystery about where Ramanujan got his equations and theorems. He had difficulty merely trying to explain how he derived his equations and found it agonizingly painful trying to develop the proofs that would ordinarily lead one to the desired result. When asked how he derived the equations, he replied that they were given to him in his dreams by the goddess Namagiri of Namakkal.

A clue that the transpersonal psyche of the ultimate reality has a message for the individual is in the experiencing of "big dreams." *Big dreams* is Jung's colloquial term for archetypal dreams that incorporate a peculiar numinosity.[342] Big dreams occasion a numinous experience that causes us to feel as if we are being visited by a consciousness different from our own. Corbett compares this experience with the analogy that just as a wave is part of the ocean, the experiencing ego is not in fact separate from the transpersonal level of consciousness.[343] These special kinds of dreams are the sources of deep religious and spiritual beliefs because they often provide a glimpse of the spirits of the recently dead, ghosts, demons, and angels, all of which are archetypal images.[344] Jeremy Taylor, a psychologist and Unitarian minister who brings a Jungian perspective to dream analysis, explains:

> Dreams always come to bring us to a deeper understanding of the Divine…There is a potentially unbroken continuity of experience stretching from the ordinary, limited awareness of "me"…all the way to a transcendent awareness of the completeness and oneness and self-identification with the ALL—the Divine.[345]

This awareness is a transpersonal moment when the individual realizes that they are experiencing something outside the boundaries of everyday ego consciousness.

Dreaming Beyond Death, by Dr. Kelley Bulkeley and Rev. Dr. Patricia Bulkeley, looks at predeath dreams. A predeath dream is a dream that occurs before one dies. Predeath dreams are seen as "powerful metaphorical expressions, as creative visions of what it will be like to pass from living to dying."[346] The authors stress that their book does not address the question of life after death nor the research done on NDEs. Its limited objective is to provide the dying person with useful knowledge about the message the dream is conveying. NDEs, by definition, do not happen to people who die, whereas predeath dreams only happen to people who *do* die. What is striking in predeath dreams are the frequent references to a special kind of light. Light is an important element in many ASCs.

Entheogens

Entheogens are psychoactive substances that bring about altered states of consciousness. Huston Smith recognized that entheogens had the ability to open the doors of perception and provide us with knowledge of ultimate reality, or as he refers to it, "the sacred unconscious."[347] However, he reminded us that even though we may experience ultimate reality, and even if such experience could be shown to be veridical, the true goal of such an experience is to move us to live a religious life.[348]

Smith viewed the term "entheogen" as preferable to "hallucinogen" or "psychedelic" because he was seeking a word that would denote virtually nonaddictive, mind-altering substances, which are employed "seriously and reverently."[349] He was curious as to whether an experience of the sacred varies depending on whether one is influenced by entheogens, so he devised a test for students at Princeton University. He presented them with two accounts of religious experiences: one under the influence of drugs and one not. Twice as many students failed to identify which was which as those who guessed correctly, leading him to conclude that there are no discernible differences between the two experiences.

Smith also undertook a study of entheogenic plants and chemicals in an attempt to determine how, if at all, they related to religion.

He ingested some capsules of mescaline in order to study the effects of that entheogen on his quest for more knowledge of the divine. He experienced an altered state of consciousness in which he discovered "about five distinguishable layers" of consciousness. He described how he experienced what is referred to as "emanationism," or a flowing out, which began with a "clear, unbroken Light of the Void."[350] He described his experience as a "distinctive blend of fear and fascination":

> The experience was momentous because it showed me range upon range of reality that previously I had only believed existed and tried without much success to imagine. Whence, then, the terror? In part, from my sense of the utter freedom of the psyche and its domination over the body. I was aware of my body, laid out on the couch as if on an undertaker's slab, cool and slightly moist. But I also had the sense that it would reactivate only if my spirit chose to reenter it. Should it so choose? There seemed to be no clear reason for it to do so.[351]

Smith is considered to have been one of the world's most influential figures in religious studies. What he has to say about entheogens is directly relevant to the ultimate reality, which is accessible in an altered state of consciousness: "The problem, or rather mystery, that stalks our understanding of the entheogens is how Ultimate Reality or God can disclose Him/her/itself—the pronouns never work—to us through changes in brain chemistry."[352] Note that Smith conflates Ultimate Reality with God, recognizing that the name is of little consequence.

Michael Pollan, a writer who explored the effects of entheogens on the "reducing valve" (Huxley's term), feels that when the ego is no longer blocking impressions and meanings during the experience of the numinosum, "what comes through...in a great flood, is love."[353] Pollan's experience agrees with that of Huxley who, after a session with LSD, stated, "What came through the closed door [of perception] was the realization...the direct total awareness, from the inside, so to say, of Love as the primary and fundamental cosmic fact."[354] Huxley described his experience as having provided him with access to "a spiritual realm of ineffable beauty." That realm is the ultimate reality.[355]

Pollan stated, after his experiences with entheogens, "The journeys have shown me what the Buddhists try to tell us, but I have never really understood: that there is much more to consciousness than the ego, as we would see if it would just shut up. And that its dissolution (or transcendence) is nothing to fear; in fact, it is a prerequisite for making any spiritual progress."[356]

Out-of-Body-Experiences (OBEs)

An OBE can thus be defined as the presence of the following three phenomenological elements:

- the feeling of being outside one's physical body (or disembodiment);

- the presence of a distanced and elevated visuospatial perspective; and

- the seeing of one's own body.[357]

Autoscopy, by contrast, is the experience of seeing oneself from outside one's own material body.[358] In an autoscopic experience, an individual sees a double of themselves without the feeling of having left one's body; it is not, therefore, an OBE but the experience of a doppelgänger.

The OBE (sometimes referred to as an exosomatic experience) is one in which consciousness separates from the material body.[359] This separation is reported in approximately 75 percent of the cases of NDEs.[360] While in this condition, the person has the experience of their consciousness existing separate from their body. Often this experience of consciousness is above the body, but may also be in locations far removed from the body.[361]

In some, but not all, out-of-body experiences, there is a silver cord that connects the nonmaterial body to the material body.[362] In those reports, it is presumed that if the cord is cut, the individual's consciousness will be unable to return to the physical body, and death will ensue.[363]

The discoveries of researchers into the phenomenon of NDEs have much in common with the teachings of Tibetan Buddhism. In Tibetan Buddhism, the NDE may be thought of as the *bardo*, which is the state of consciousness between the two realities of life and death.[364] Sogyal Rinpoche, a Tibetan lama, explains:

> It is at this point that consciousness leaves the body and continues its journey into the Bardo of becoming. It now possesses a "mental body" that has a number of characteristics: It is very light and lucid, the consciousness is nine times clearer than in earthly life, and it possesses clairvoyance and other miraculous powers. This body is similar to the body

of the previous existence, but perfectly complete and in the prime of life.[365]

The OBE, which is a characteristic of many NDEs, suggests the existence of a "subtle body," a nonmaterial consciousness that exists independent of the body. This subtle body, variously called an astral body, a resurrection body, an immortal body, or a diamond body, is a topic worthy of discussion, for it may provide further evidence of the nonmaterial aspect of ultimate reality.

This etheric double (astral, mental) of a person might involve characteristics or aspects of an unknown part of the electromagnetic continuum—or perhaps from a low magnitude of light not yet accessible to current technology: "Finally, energetic doubles might constitute evidence for a fifth force in nature that in principle could be integrated with the current four forces into a unified model."[366] Annie Besant puts it this way:

> But when we come to look at an advanced soul, it is this and the one above it that at once strike the eye as being emphatically the presentation of the man; radiant in light, most glorious and delicate in coloring, showing hues that no language can describe, because they have no place in earth's spectrum—hues not only the most pure and beautiful, but entirely different from the colors known on the lower planes, additional ones which show the growth of the man in those higher regions in the loftier qualities and powers that there exist.[367]

As consciousness pervades many of the topics in this book, such as in out-of-body experiences, near-death experiences, or altered states of consciousness, it is important to reconsider the dualism question. The problem of how the body and mind interact applies to both the Western and Eastern concepts, but in different ways. At its most basic level, body/mind dualism may be described as the problem of how abstract entities such as thoughts and ideas arise from neurons or a bundle of perceptions. Conversely, how do thoughts influence neurons and thus affect our bodies?[368] Some attempts to explain these problems are found in philosophical discussions of dualism, bundle theory, and idealism, some of which have support in one or more Buddhist traditions.

Dualism, which I briefly mentioned in the previous chapter, is a philosophical term that holds that the mind and body are, in some unknown way, separate from each other.[369] An early proponent of the notion was Aristotle, who assumed that if the mind was capable of receiving all kinds of data (unlike the eyes, which receive only visible data), it must, therefore, be immaterial. However, it was René Descartes, a French rationalist philosopher, who was largely responsible for the form dualism has taken up to the current day. He is widely remembered for his proclamation *"Cogito ergo sum,"* which translates to "I think; therefore I am." His revolutionary "Cogito" was constructed after he began to investigate how the body and mind interact. He reasoned that while he could doubt he had a body; he could not doubt that he had a mind. "Cartesian dualism" was thus born and became, and continues to be, an important topic of debate.

Descartes's view of the mind/body relationship is often referred to as "substance dualism," which holds that the mind is "an independently existing substance" that does not have extension in space. Substance dualism holds that "immortal souls occupy an independent 'realm' of existence separate and distinct from that of the physical world"[370] (see Kastrup's view of this in the preceding chapter). While Descartes considered body and mind to be two different substances, the Dutch philosopher Spinoza considered body and mind to simply be different aspects of one reality. I argue throughout this book that there is but one reality, which is the ultimate reality that manifests in different ways in our objective, perceptual reality.[371] Karl Popper noted that before Descartes, most important philosophers were either implicitly or explicitly dualistic interactionists, so in that sense, Descartes had followed them.[372]

Philosopher David Hume came after Descartes. He rejected Cartesian dualism, arguing instead for a "bundle theory" to explain the body/mind problem. This theory held that there were conscious mental states involving thoughts, sensations, emotions, and so on, but no "Self" over and above those states. In other words, Hume held that the whole is nothing more than the sum of its parts, and therefore there is no Self.[373] Hume argued that if you take away the descriptive terms of an object, there is nothing left. He offered the example of an apple. It may be round, shiny, red, and sweet, but if you take away those qualities, there is nothing left. He went on to say that individuals were the same: "Our senses are just floating simultaneously arranged together to form who we are." Hume's bundle theory is remarkably similar to the Buddhist doctrine of "anattā," or no-self, causing one to question just how influential that Buddhist doctrine was to Hume.[374]

Although dualism has intuitive appeal, a major criticism of it is that if mind and body are two separate kinds of things, how can any interaction take place between them? Jung's student C. A. Meier suggested that where the mind and the body come together is through the phenomenon of synchronicity, which I discussed in Chapter 3.

Although Jung took exception to the view that synchronicity could account for the connection of the body and mind,[375] both he and von Franz considered it a fact that the unconscious is connected with matter, in agreement with dualism.[376]

A more recent critic of dualism is philosopher Daniel Dennett. Dennett's book *Consciousness Explained* has a chapter titled "Why Dualism is Forlorn" in which he argues:

> The prevailing wisdom, variously expressed and argued for is materialism: there is one sort of stuff, namely matter—the physical stuff of physics, chemistry, and physiology—and the mind is somehow nothing but a physical phenomenon. In short, the mind is the brain.[377]

He attempts to support his idea that the mind is the brain by noting the conflict between standard physics and dualism, concluding that the principle of the conservation of energy is the "inescapable flaw in dualism." Henry Stapp, a theoretical physicist, argues that the problem with his statement is that while it may be true within the "standard physics" rubric, "the argument collapses when one goes over to contemporary physics…Contemporary physical theory allows, and its orthodox von Neumann form entails, an interactive dualism that is fully in accord with all the laws of physics."[378]

Stapp has also recognized the problems inherent in trying to understand how two such different realms can be connected. He notes that "contemporary physics is essentially dualistic," but because it supports dualism, it is summarily scorned.[379] Nonetheless, quantum physics provides empirical evidence as to how these two seemingly opposite attributes of living things may, in fact, be linked.

Freeman Dyson, a theoretical physicist and mathematician, considered consciousness to be more than just a physical activity of a brain. He felt that mind was inherent in every electron, arguing that human consciousness was only different in degree, not in kind.[380]

If we assume that atoms have no physical properties, as Heisenberg claimed, and acknowledge that molecules are comprised of atoms, and that we in turn are comprised of molecules, do we have any physical properties? It is not a leap in logic to conclude that the claims of dualism may be false, but in an unexpected way: there may be no material realm! Our perceptive reality may prove to be illusory, as suggested by Plato and Eastern philosophy. Heisenberg's statement about the absence of physical properties of the atom provides an argument by which to criticize materialists such as Dennett: there may be only one realm for both mind and body, and that realm may not be physical. Nonmaterial aspects of the human body have been mentioned in many Platonic dialogues, but one that is particularly interesting comes from the *Phaedo*:

> And indeed the soul reasons best when none of these senses troubles it, neither hearing nor sight, not pain nor pleasure, but when it is most by itself, taking leave of the body and as far as possible having no contact or association with it in its search for reality.[381]

This observation of Plato that "the soul reasons best when none of the senses troubles it" agrees with what Susan Blackmore reports of the similarities in lucid dreams and NDEs in the following pages: "Consciousness is often reported as extremely clear in both."

The nonmaterial body is also mentioned in the New Testament's 1 Corinthians 15:44, where Paul states, "It is sown as a natural body; it is raised a spiritual body. There is a natural body, and there is a spiritual body." As one would expect with the interpretation of scripture, there is no unanimity over Paul's meaning.

The idea that humans consist of both a soul and a material body is an age-old idea of peoples all over the world. Some philosophers have even posited a third component: "an astral body, meaning literally 'starry body,' and sometimes called 'the body of light.' This astral body is an exact copy of the flesh and blood body and is made of finer material."[382] Marie-Louis von Franz, a collaborator with the Swiss psychologist Carl Jung, considered the subtle body to be a form of the psyche:

> That would indeed remain close to the body but would also still possess a certain minimal mass and extension in time-space, a form of appearance which admittedly would no longer be understood as physical in the ordinary sense of the word.[383]

Psychologist von Franz notes that in modern physics, mass is no longer associated with a material substance, and hence particles are not seen as consisting of any basic "stuff," but as bundles of energy."[384] Her observation agrees with that of Heisenberg.

There are many anecdotal reports that claim that the astral or subtle body is a distinctive feature of many NDEs.[385] Clearly some sort of dualist theory is a prerequisite for considering the possibility that a nonmaterial body can have an existence independent of the physical body. Some writers refer to this nonmaterial body as the "etheric body" and consider it to be the same as the so-called "astral body," but as Blackmore notes, theosophical tradition considers them as distinctly different. The etheric body is described as physical in some fashion; the astral body is described as finer than the etheric body. According to theosophical thought, all physical objects have their astral double on the astral plane.[386]

Blackmore defines OBEs as *experiences*, adding, "It does not imply any particular *interpretation* of the OBE. There may or may not be a double, something may or may not leave the body; the definition presupposes none of these possibilities."[387] She goes on to say, "[T]he *experience* of being out of the body is not equivalent to the *fact* of being out."[388] This distinction between a factual occurrence and an experience, however, means very little to the individual who has the experience. In fact, I would argue, except for any effect on the physical world left by an occurrence such as an OBE, there is no real difference. Making a distinction between subjective and objective realities may only be necessary in the limited case where the subjective experience acts upon, or influences in some way, objective reality.

Dianne Edgcombe offers a slightly different interpretation of an OBE. She describes it as: "An altered state of consciousness in which the subject feels that his mind or sense of self-awareness is separated from his physical body and that his sense of self-awareness is more vivid and more real than a dream."[389] Edgcombe also notes that although the majority of the scientific and medical communities regard such events as simply hallucinations, "a growing minority view argues that they may be evidence of another reality."[390] This minority view is shared by Physicist Fred Alan Wolf, whom I previously quoted as saying, with respect to dreams, "Such dreams are actually visits to parallel realities."

Lucid dreams and OBEs are considered by LaBerge to be merely different interpretations of the same phenomenon.[391] Ann Faraday, in agreement with both LaBerge and Celia Green, holds "that it is not possible to discuss lucid dreams without considering their relation to out-of-body experiences."[392] Edgcombe, however, disagrees with the idea that lucid dreams and OBEs are just different interpretations of the same phenomena. She has experienced both OBEs and lucid dreams, and in her dissertation she argues that lucid dreams differ from OBEs:

> My lucid dreams feel unreal whereas my OBEs feel real. When I experienced my OBEs, I felt that I was experiencing reality, the same way I experience everyday reality. During my lucid dreams, even though I was aware, I was aware that I was dreaming: I knew that the experience was not real.[393]

Blackmore has studied both lucid dreams and OBEs, and notes their many similarities:[394]

- Consciousness is often reported as extremely clear in both.

- In both, perception can be described as clearer and more vivid than in normal perception.

- Both are sometimes described as being profound and life-altering experiences.

- People often strive to have more of them.

- The simplifications, distortions, and additions found in the experienced world can be similar in both experiences.

- In both, imagining or thinking about changes in the environment can bring about those changes.

- Flying is common in both.

- In both, there are oddities of lighting such as self-illumination of objects and the difficulty of switching lights on.

There is one important difference between lucid dreams and OBEs. Lucid dreamers are (by definition) aware that they are dreaming and therefore assume that the surroundings are not real, whereas OBErs are often convinced that their surroundings *are* real. Exploring the reports of experiences of lucid dreams, OBEs, NDEs, and other altered states of consciousness may help us understand even more about the nature of ultimate reality.

Near-Death Experiences

There are literally thousands of reports of NDEs, and although they are considered anecdotal by many, their significance lies in their strong similarities, irrespective of cultural influences or religious beliefs.

One of the earliest reports of a NDE is that of a man called Er, as told by Plato. He had supposedly died in a war and was picked up on the battlefield along with his dead comrades ten days later. He was then taken home to be prepared for his funeral. On the twelfth day, when he lay upon the funeral pyre, he revived and reported what he had seen in the world of the dead. He described traveling with others to a "marvelous place" where he encountered judges. The just were instructed to enter the door on the right to go to heaven, and those who were deemed unjust were to travel downward through the opening on the left.[395] To Plato, birth is when the sleeping begins, because the soul is coming from a much greater state of awareness (this is a commonly described attribute of the NDE): "Death, by implication, is an *awakening* and *remembering*."[396]

NDEs differ from dreams and hallucinations because they appear to reflect an underlying structure. There are notable differences in individuals' perceptions during NDEs that are unique to the individual.[397] Also, if the reality experienced in an NDE is so wonderful that people do not want to return, one has to wonder: What is the purpose of the embodiment of the soul, spirit, consciousness, or whatever? Why do we have an existence on the material plane? David Chalmers asks, "Why are we conscious?"[398] but others, drawing on the reports of those who have experienced the blissful states of NDEs and OBEs, question, "Why are we embodied?" Lee Irwin, a retired professor of religious studies, has an idea about that. He feels that embodiment is "crucial for the actualization of deep consciousness potential,"[399] without elaborating on exactly what that means.

Blackmore's argument as to the important differences between OBEs and lucid dreams shares a similarity with the claim that NDEs are dreams. Psychologist Ring and pediatric professor Sharon Cooper are adamant in their view that the NDE is not a dream but is an entirely novel example of how ultimate reality manifests in our experiences. They cite, as examples, the NDEs reported by congenitally blind individuals:

> These excerpts make it abundantly clear that from our respondents' point of view, the NDE, especially its visual aspect, has nothing in common with their usual dreams. It is instead something sui generis, and not to be conflated with dreams. Since there

is no support whatever from our interviews for the dream hypothesis of NDEs, we may confidently reject it as a potential explanation for our findings.[400]

An important reason to study the NDE lies in its ability to aid individuals through the grieving process.[401] To some, an even more important reason is the possibility that NDEs provide a glimpse of what to expect after death.

At the time of his writing the landmark work *Life after Life*, Dr. Raymond Moody was familiar with 150 cases that fall under the rubric of NDE. He was able to separate those cases into three categories:

1. The experiences of persons who were resuscitated after having been thought, adjudged, or pronounced clinically dead by their doctors.

2. The experiences of persons who, in the course of accidents or severe injury or illness, came very close to physical death.

3. The experiences of persons who, as they died, told them to other people who were present. Later, these other people reported the content of the death experience to me.[402]

Although many reported aspects of the experience are ineffable, there are some characteristics that Moody found were common in reports of NDEs. Among these are encountering a dark tunnel; meeting others, including a being of light; and the lasting effects such experiences have on the lives of those who have had an NDE.[403]

Moody provides many other examples of reports of NDEs in his fascinating study. Others who, following Moody's lead, have studied the phenomenon have noted characteristics of the experience similar to those reported by Moody.

Another interesting fact about the NDE was observed by Stafford Betty, a professor of world religions. Betty noted that Alzheimer's patients showed terminal lucidity just before death. They were often able to speak rationally when they had been unable to speak for years. It remains a mystery as to how that was possible with a deteriorated brain—unless the brain's function differs from what is generally accepted.[404]

One NDE that I consider important for several reasons is that of a patient of Dr. Michael Sabom, a cardiologist. In his book he recounts the story of Pam Reynolds, a woman who was undergoing a surgical procedure for the excision of a basilar artery aneurysm. In order to perform the delicate operation, her body temperature was lowered to sixty degrees Fahrenheit. Both her heartbeat and breathing ceased, and blood was completely drained from her head. Her EEG showed flat readings—a symptom of brain death. However, while under these conditions of brain death, she reported having experienced classic components of an NDE, including a tunnel, an extremely bright light that she described as bright as a thousand suns at the end of the tunnel, and seeing deceased relatives, including a distant cousin whose death she had been unaware of. What makes this case significant is the doctor's confirmation that there was no brain activity possible during the experience.[405]

As with many reported NDEs, the case of Pam Reynolds is not without its detractors. Gerald M. Woerlee, an anesthesiologist,[406] has attacked Sabom's report with several arguments:

- He argues the auditory reports that she made during the time she was under the combination of drugs she was given are explainable without reference to anything out of the ordinary.

• He also recounts a personal account of a physician reported in a book published in 1895, wherein the physician describes his experience under the influence of morphine. He noted that the drug's influence elicited experiences were similar to those reported in NDEs. He concludes from that report that since opiates can induce hallucinations of transcendence, peacefulness, meeting deceased relatives, etc., that the experiences of Pam Reynolds shed no light on the possibility of the separation of body and spirit in NDEs.

These two arguments against the reality of the NDE experience can be rebutted on at least two grounds:

• Perceptions of NDE experiencers is much more involved than merely hearing conversations in the operating room. Individuals who have claimed they left their bodies during the NDE have witnessed events in waiting rooms outside the OR, including several reports of perceptions outside the hospital (see below). Furthermore, Greyson has noted that "[t]here is no convincing evidence for adequately anesthetized patients having any explicit, or conscious, memory of events during the surgery (apart from patients who have reported such memories in connection with an NDE)."[407]

• With regard to the reported experience of the physician under the influence of morphine, I have previously argued that correlations do not equate with cause. It may be that experiences of those under the influence of mind-altering drugs are due to the effect of the drugs on the "filtering" function of the brain. Perceptions under the influence of mind-altering drugs may be providing access to a transcendental realm, or ultimate reality, in the same way as does the NDE: through a reduction in the filtering function of the brain. This does not mean that the experience of such realm is not "real." Pam Reynold's brain had been completely emptied of blood, and there was no movement on the EEG; her brain's filtering function was therefore incapable of blocking any perception of a transcendental realm.

It is also worth noting that comparing the experiences of those who have had an NDE with individuals who have had similar experiences while under the influence of mind-altering drugs neglects the effect of the experience on the individuals. Those who have had an NDE become changed individuals: they have no doubt of the reality of the experience or its importance. One individual who had experienced a hallucination while under the influence of codeine from a previous hospital stay said, "[T]his experience was nothing like the hallucinations, nothing like them at all."[408]

The sense of reality experienced in NDEs has been called "realer than real." An integrated study combining psychodynamic and electrophysiological approaches suggests such descriptions may be accurate. In a recent attempt to understand more about NDEs, a group of scientists armed with information from EEGs and the neural markers found that "NDE memories were significantly different from memories of imagined events," and concluded that "at a phenomenological level, NDE memories cannot be considered equivalent to imagined memories, and at a neural level, NDE memories are stored as episodic memories of events experienced in a peculiar state of consciousness."[409]

NDEs differ from experiences under the influence of mind-altering drugs in an important way. Although the sensory stimuli reported in NDEs and under the influence of drugs has been compared in an effort to equate the two experiences, they are qualitatively different. Those who have experienced an NDE have lost their fear of death. Also, upon returning to their bodies, they have been angry at having returned—they are resentful for having been saved.

Attempts to explain NDEs and OBEs come under three main headings: psychological, physiological, and nonmaterial or transcendental.[410] In the Christian Bible and the Koran of the Muslims, the spiritual beings encountered by prophets or devotees are considered to be "real," as opposed to hallucinations. In contrast, *The Tibetan Book of the Dead* strongly argues that "every vision, without any exception whatsoever…is purely illusionary."[411] There is a distinction between the "beings" seen in an NDE and the experience of seeing one's own body. Sabom labels the NDE in which the individual sees their own body as an "autoscopic" NDE.[412] "Autoscopy," as I mentioned earlier, is "[t]he experience of hallucination in which one sees oneself from outside one's own body." The disconnect here is that while "hallucination" is defined as "[p]erception of visual, auditory, tactile, olfactory, or gustatory stimuli in the absence of any external objects or events," the perception of one's body lying on the operating table isn't in "the absence of any external objects."

The perception of otherworldly beings during an NDE may be hallucinations, but perceiving one's own body during such an experience does not meet the definition of hallucination, especially where the perception of medical procedures done in the operating room is confirmed by doctors and other medical personnel.[413] Sabom recounts the story of a young woman who had an NDE as a result of being hit by a car. She reported that she was watching what the medics were doing to her body and noted that the new dress she was wearing was ruined. She described her mental state as "devoid of emotion"; she was not frightened. Thirteen years after that accident, Dr. Sabom interviewed her, and she claimed that she could now leave her body at will—that she had somehow learned how to do that from her NDE.[414] It may be similar to situations in which we are sure we can't do something, but then when we try to do it, we find that we can and are left to wonder why we ever doubted our ability.

The beings, including dead relatives, reported being seen by those experiencing an NDE may be hallucinations. There is no way to confirm the reality of such images. Anecdotal reports of collective apparitions—that is, apparitions seen by two or more individuals— may offer some evidence that the beings seen in NDEs are more than hallucinations. One example of such an apparition is recounted by Thomas Tietze, former professor of parapsychology at the University of Minnesota:

> Two brothers, occupying a cabin in an old-time na-
> val ship, were sleeping in cots hung parallel to one
> another. Both brothers must have been awakened
> suddenly and simultaneously—by what they never
> knew—by some irresistible and unknown power—
> to see standing between their cots the figure of
> their father. Both gazed in mute amazement: there
> it stood, motionless for a moment, which seemed a
> century; then it raised one hand and pointed to its
> own eyes. They were closed. My brother, says the

narrator, started up in bed, and as he did so the form vanished. Their father died at about that time.[415]

Another account of collective apparitions is related by Colin Wilson. It concerns two principals of Oxford College who, in a 1901 visit to Versailles, witnessed a period of time from the age of Marie Antoinette, the late 1700s. During the experience, they felt "oddly depressed and experienced a 'dreamlike' sensation." Wilson relates more tales of a similar nature, providing unanswered questions about the nature of such visions.[416]

Some have suggested that NDEs can be caused by ketamine, which is a drug used to begin and maintain anesthesia. This so-called ketamine model of NDEs has been the subject of research of Karl Jansen, MD, PhD. After several years researching the possibility that ketamine was instrumental in causing NDEs, Jansen concluded, "Ketamine is a door to a place we cannot normally get to; it is definitely not evidence that such a place does not exist."[417] The place to which Jansen refers is ultimate reality.

The quantum theory of multiverses might explain OBEs and NDEs—the other universes visited in such states may just be "non-consensual realties," such as those we visit in dreams. This may be a reasonable explanation due to the fact that when someone is having an OBE, the immediate vicinity of where they are when the OBE occurs seems to be a very true representation of the consensual reality they experience in their normal state. However, as they move further from their body, there becomes discrepancies between their everyday waking reality and what they are experiencing. It may be the case that there is a consensual reality interwoven into everyday reality, but in the altered universe of the OBE, there is no one to "provide consensus" to the experience. However if, during the experience, they meet someone who perceives them, then there becomes a consensus, and verifiable information can be obtained that supports the validity of the experience.

Validating OBE and NDE experiences is understandably problematic. Those reports that are thought to provide proof of the existence of a nonmaterial body are not without valid criticisms. Much of the research is based upon reports that are largely anecdotal. Nevertheless, I am including some of the more interesting reports. The lack of veridicality may be due to the fact that the astral body is not in a consensual reality...the experience may be just as real, and in some cases even more real, to the individual, regardless of whether or not it is "veridical." Notably, those who have experienced an out-of-body experience claim that the experience is as different from dreams or the experience of mind-altering drugs, as is the difference between dreams and waking states.[418]

The memory of an NDE continues for years. It often changes one's attitudes and perspectives on life. After Ernest Hemingway had an NDE during a battle in Italy in World War I, he wrote to his parents, "Dying is a very simple thing. I've looked at death, and I really know. If I should have died it would have been...quite the easiest thing I ever did." Hemingway incorporated his memory of his NDE in his short story "The Snows of Kilimanjaro" and in his major novel *A Farewell to Arms.* [419]

Two elements of reported NDEs are worthy of further investigation: perceptions while in the near-death state and the nature of the light seen during an NDE.

The perceptions of those who experience either an OBE or NDE are often remarkable. Senses are reported to be enhanced when in an out-of-body state. Green reports that in some cases, the subjects' senses are restored if they had any sensory deprivation such as poor eyesight or deafness. She includes a case in which the subject, experiencing an OBE, had entered the room of a niece: "By her bedside was an open book, and I found no difficulty in reading the two open pages (which would have been impossible in my physical body, without my glasses)."[420]

Van Lommel recounts reports of NDEs that purport to show that out-of-body perceptions were completely accurate in approximately 90 percent of the cases studied, with 8 percent containing some minor error and 2 percent entirely incorrect. He concludes from this study "that an OBE cannot be a hallucination, that is, the experiencing of a perception that has no basis in 'reality,' like in psychosis; neither can it be a delusion, which is an incorrect assessment of a correct perception, nor an illusion, which means a misapprehension or misleading image."[421]

Moody and Long and many others who have investigated NDEs mention light as being an important element of NDEs. In fact, some researchers claim that the light seen by those who experience an NDE is the key element in an NDE and one that cannot be accounted for by neuroscience.[422] Morse quotes those who have experienced an NDE as describing it as "all-forgiving," "all-loving," and misty like a "glowing cloud."[423] This light is also described as conveying a feeling of love and also warmth.[424] If the light gives a feeling of warmth, then we can assume that the person (entity, spirit, and soul) experiencing the NDE was lower in temperature: if the light and the individual were of the same temperature, there would be no sensation of warmth coming from the light.

Since light is so important to those who describe their NDE, it warrants further investigation. Thanks to a teaching experiment designed by Arthur Zajonc, a physics professor at Amherst College, we know that if there is no material object upon which light can reflect, then all is dark. The exhibition created by Zajonc involved a box into which light can be shone directly without illuminating any objects in the box or interior surfaces of the box itself. The exhibition showed that although light filled the box, it could not be seen unless it struck an object.[425] Since experiencers of NDEs are in a realm without material objects, the question arises as to what is making the light visible. The light must be self-generated and not reflected since there is nothing material off which it can reflect.

This same strange light is described by Pollan while under the influence of entheogens:

> And then there was this light, it was the pure light of love and divinity, and it was with me and no words were needed. I was in the presence of this absolute pure divine love and I was merging with it, in this explosion of energy.[426]

Huxley, also under the influence of entheogens, stated, "First and most important is the experience of light."[427]

Hypnosis

Hypnosis is an altered state of consciousness that differs from other ASCs in that generally one is placed into the state of hypnosis by the act of someone else. This difference and the behavior of those under the influence of hypnosis have caused some psychologists and philosophers to question whether hypnosis is, in fact, an ASC.[428]

Nevertheless, there are several attributes of the hypnotic state that are of interest. There have been numerous reports of individuals undergoing surgery in an induced hypnotic state without the experience or memory of pain. Even Freud voiced some confusion about the nature of hypnosis after witnessing a man's arm being blistered by a piece of ice after having been given the suggestion under hypnosis that it was, in fact, a red-hot poker.[429]

An interesting report on a hypnotic experience was recounted by Thomson Jay Hudson in his early book *The Law of Psychic Phenomena.* Hudson reports that he once saw an individual placed under hypnosis whom he described as "a cultured gentleman, possessed of a decided taste for philosophical studies, and was a graduate of a leading college…[and] a decided unbeliever in modern spiritism."[430] The gentleman, under the influence of hypnosis and referred to merely as "C," was asked how he would like to have a personal interview with Socrates, given the man's interest in philosophy. C acknowledged that he would consider it a great privilege if Socrates were alive. The professor who was conducting the hypnosis demonstration then told C that he could invoke Socrates's spirit. Pointing to a corner of the room, he exclaimed, "There he stands now." C looked toward the corner of the room and exhibited a look of "reverential awe." C was then assured that Socrates was willing to answer any question put to him by C, and C at once began to question Socrates in a session that lasted over two hours: "His questions embraced the whole cosmogony of the universe and a wide range of spiritual philosophy." According to Hudson, the information which came from the interview with Socrates "the whole philosophy was such a coherent system…it could have been printed in a book verbatim and would have formed one of the grandest and most coherent systems of spiritual philosophy ever conceived by the brain of man."[431]

At a subsequent séance, C, once again under hypnosis, was introduced to a "pig," who he was told was a reincarnation of a Hindu priest whose karma had gotten him into this form, but who retained "a perfect recollection of his former incarnation, and had

not forgotten his learning." Needless to say, the "pig" was as knowledgeable as had been Socrates.[432]

The relevance of these demonstrations of hypnosis is not to show
that Socrates or the reincarnated Hindu had, in fact, been contacted,
but rather to support Hudson's claim that man had "two minds,"
one of which had far greater powers than the other. The objective
mind relied on the five senses to deal with perceptual reality; the
subjective mind operated independently of the senses. It may be that
when an individual is in a hypnotic state, the subjective mind is able
to manifest intuition, which Hudson claimed functioned at a high
level when the objective mind was arrested. Somehow, when in a
somnambulistic state, the subjective mind could draw "upon a power
and energy far greater than the subject could exercise by conscious
effort."[433] In this somnambulistic state, there is the possibility that
there is some softening of the boundaries between the objective
and subjective, the perceptual reality and the ultimate reality. This
"softening" of the boundaries between objective and subjective reality was mentioned in the discussion of lucid dreams, so in that sense
there may be a relationship between the two experiences. It is also
possible that hypnosis has the ability to affect the brain's filter, as
has been previously discussed. More study of the subject of hypnosis
must be done in order to better understand the nature of the experience, and how such an experience can help us further understand
consciousness and the mind.

Having examined consciousness and altered states of consciousness, the next step is to consider what happens to consciousness when
the body perishes.

7

The Continuation of Consciousness

Où Allons Nous

No one knows with regard to death whether it is not really the greatest blessing that can happen to man; but people dread it as though they were certain it is the greatest evil.

—Plato

After death you will be what you were before your birth.

—Arthur Schopenhauer

It is impossible that anything so natural, so necessary and so universal as death, should ever have been designed by providence as an evil to mankind.

—Jonathan Swift

GAUGUIN WONDERED, LIKE MANY OF us, "where do we go" when we "shuffle off this mortal coil." Jung claimed he did not have the answer but felt that it was important for everyone to develop some kind of belief or understanding about the question of immortality.[434]

Death is the end of life for the body; transcendence is the passing of a soul or spirit into a realm beyond perceptual reality. In Hoffman's metaphor of computer icons, discussed in Chapter 4, transcendence may be thought of as moving from the desktop to the recycle bin. The "real" individual, who interfaces with the everyday reality we experience, can be likened to the file, which the icon (the body) represents. Moving the icon to the recycle bin does not delete the file; it merely removes it from view.

Some philosophers distinguish between the terms "transcendence" and "immortality," noting that transcendence suggests a continuation of existence after death, which may be of limited duration, whereas immortality implies continuation of the person in some form for eternity. Furthermore, if ultimate reality is outside of space and time, as some who have experienced ASCs claim, can we even begin to comprehend what it would be like to spend "eternity" in *any* state of existence? Is "eternity" a meaningful concept if it is outside space and time?

It is important at the outset of a discussion on transcendence to recall what was said about dualism. Dualism is the argument that we are embodied nonphysical minds or souls, and as such, the destruction of the physical body does not necessarily destroy us as persons. Dualism does not, however, require that we survive bodily death. The soul or mind may have the ability to separate from the body, as in an OBE, but it may be dependent on the body and cease when the body is destroyed. Materialism, on the other hand, rules out any hope for survival with the exception of the Christian theology of resurrection.

Reports of those who have had an NDE provide no evidence for the nature of the afterlife for the reason that, by their very nature, they are *near-death* experiences.

There are two important questions concerning the fate of the soul after death:

1. Does the soul cease to exist?

2. If it does not cease to exist, what is the nature of its existence beyond the world of perceptions?

One group that believes the soul does not cease to exist consists of those who claim to have communicated with the dead. Such anecdotal, apocryphal claims are problematic and are often dismissed out of hand as "nonsense." Nonetheless, they do deserve to be considered with an open mind.

William James, whom I have previously introduced, was very open minded to the idea that we survive death. He was a member of the Society for Psychical Research along with such luminaries as Tennyson, Thomson (discoverer of the electron), Mark Twain, Lewis Carroll, and others.[435] Although James was curious and open minded, he was not gullible. James attended many "sittings" with a Mrs. Piper, who claimed to be a medium in contact with a spirit called Hodson, who had been a close friend of James's while he was alive. James expressed serious doubts about the veracity of the claims of Mrs. Piper.

In one of his last comments about the possibility of surviving death, James wrote, "I therefore repeat that if ever our growing familiarity with these phenomena should tend more and more to corroborate the hypothesis that 'spirits' play some part in their production, I shall be quite ready to undeaden my ears and to revoke the negative conclusions of this limited report."[436] James concluded, "the Creator has eternally intended this department of nature to remain *baffling*... [such experiences] can never be fully explained away, they can also never be susceptible to full corroboration."[437]

Colin Wilson, drawing on his extensive research on the afterlife, has concluded:

> We are inclined to think of death either as a dead end, or as a launching into a totally new kind of existence: some strange mystical state in which all the secrets of the universe will be known. All the evidence we have considered indicates that this is a misconception. Life on the "next plane" is apparently not fundamentally dissimilar from life on earth, although many of its conditions seem to be different...the individual survives death in a form not unlike his present mode of being.[438]

Plato's *Phaedo* recounts Socrates's argument for immortality. Socrates sought to convince his fellow Greeks of immortality through the application of logic. He attempted to show that immortality is true, and that the belief is, therefore, rational. He began by assuming that the soul does exist. He developed his argument to show, through reason, that the soul is immortal. To do this, he argued that everything has an opposite: when we awake, we were previously asleep; when we sleep, we will awake again; something that becomes hot was previously cold, and so on. Being alive is the opposite of being dead, and since death comes from life, life must come from death (see Schopenhauer's quote above).

Some philosophers are quick to point out obvious problems with Plato's theory of opposites. For one thing, it is clear that there are many "things" that don't have an opposite, like a refrigerator. But such criticism misses the point. Socrates is talking about something intangible: the soul. It is, I believe, more appropriate to apply Socrates's argument to the intangible states of mind such as love, hate, appreciation of beauty, and so on. Even his analogy of hot and cold reflects a perception by the nonmaterial mind. Many states of mind do, in fact, have opposites. His argument from opposites deserves to be taken seriously.

Moody, whose work I have discussed throughout this book, identified some of the problems inherent to reincarnation:

> [S]omething like reincarnation poses certain obstacles to observation. Where does the soul go when it is between bodies? What is the evidence for a different plane of being where souls reside waiting for a physical incarnation? Why aren't we consciously aware of having lived before?[439]

The first question Moody asks, "Where does the soul go when it is between bodies?" is described in *The Tibetan Book of the Dead*. Buddhism holds that the state of existence between reincarnations is not just one state. There are "three principal types of *bardos* related to the process of death and rebirth: the bardo of the moment of dying, the bardo of *dharmatā* "in which there is blinding light, and overwhelming illumination"[440] [see the previous chapter's discussion on light in NDEs], and the bardo of becoming," which involves the "assessment of one's life and ends with one making one's way toward rebirth."[441] When the soul has completed its time in the in-between state, usually a forty-nine day period, it reincarnates. This after-death state in Tibetan Buddhism is described as an existence in a "prolonged dream state," which follows from the equally illusory "living state." This "dream state" is, as I have previously noted, an altered state of consciousness. The Tibetan view of the after-death state also incorporates the idea of an astral body[442] and a somewhat complicated and contradictory idea of the Self.[443] To the Tibetan Buddhist, both the living state and the dream state are equally illusory. The nature of the after-death state shows considerable variance in the Eastern philosophical and religious traditions of Confucianism, Taoism, Buddhism, and Hinduism.[444], [445]

Regression Hypnosis

What happens between death and rebirth was the subject of the book *Life Between Life*, by Toronto psychiatrist Joel Whitton and journalist Joe Fisher. Their book was hailed as the first serious work to investigate the bardo. Their research relied upon the questionable technique of regression hypnosis to discover the nature of the existence of souls between incarnations. They argued, like Plato and Schopenhauer, that life after death of the body was like the life before birth. Although Dr. Whitton's subjects had varied religious backgrounds and varied prejudices for and against the idea of reincarnation, they told him that at death, the soul leaves the body and enters a state of existence outside of space and time. Their recent life is then evaluated, and their next incarnation, taking into consideration their accumulated karma, is planned.[446]

Information about prior lives revealed when under hypnosis is, however, problematic for many reasons. Its history is particularly marred by one famous case in 1952 that was reported in the book *The Search for Bridey Murphy*, by businessman and occult enthusiast

Morey Bernstein. That book, which became an international best seller published in thirty languages, chronicled the reports of a twenty-nine-year-old married woman named Virginia Tighe. A newspaper investigated the prior life reported by Tighe, who had claimed to have remembered being born in Ireland in 1798. The paper discovered numerous inconsistencies in Tighe's account of her prior life and some facts from her current life, which seemed to suggest that she had constructed the whole thing, perhaps due to the influence of an overzealous hypnotist. The exposé of the problems with Tighe's story was itself found to contain major errors, leaving the veracity of Tighe's account of a prior life unresolved.[447]

Michael Newton, a counseling psychologist, also specialized in hypnotic regression. He professed that through hypnosis, he could take subjects back to their mother's womb, enable them to visualize past life death scenes, identify soul mates, and review past life incarnations.

The use of regression hypnosis to enable individuals to remember their birth and their prior lives has been severely criticized.[448] One study determined that verbal suggestions could easily influence a subject to create a memory of a past life. The author of the study noted that the hypnotic state occurs naturally—for example, when we hear something or see something but fail to process it consciously. Hypnosis may bring that unconscious material to consciousness, where it is misinterpreted as a factual history of the individual.[449]

Mirrors as Portals

An interesting paper, written by a museum curator and two professors of anthropology and titled *Mirrors, Portals, and Multiple Realities*, investigated the cross-culturally common mystical experience that they call *portalling*. Portalling is the experience of leaving one reality and accessing another. The experience can be evoked, they argue, in shamanistic and meditative practices by focusing one's attention on a portalling device such as a mirror. They concluded that mirrors are widespread among the world's cultures, and not just as symbolic portals, but as devices to create the interreality experience.[450] Mirrors have long occupied a place in mystical literature, and along with reflecting "cauldrons, bowls, basins, cups, and other vessels filled with liquid."[451]

I was fortunate to have Dr. Raymond Moody as one of my professors in graduate school. He is one of the most knowledgeable individuals in the field of paranormal phenomena, having coined the term "near-death experiences" in his landmark book *Life after Life*. He, like James, is not gullible. Moody, who holds both a PhD in philosophy and an MD, had observed that many near-death experiences featured visionary encounters with deceased loved ones and sought a way in which he could "trigger" such experiences under controlled conditions. He felt that if he could do that, it might be possible to help individuals with their grieving process and also perhaps learn more about the phenomenon.[452] In order to do this, he built a special room called a "psychomanteum."

The idea for such a room came from Moody's research into the Greek Oracle of the Dead at Ephyra, as described by Plato in the *Republic*. A psychomanteum is a room set up in such a way as to allow an individual to gaze into a mirror tilted to prevent them from seeing their reflection. The room is dimly lit with a light behind the individual.[453] Experiences in a psychomanteum bear a striking resemblance to that of portalling described in *Mirrors, Portals, and Multiple Realities*. Moody's description of the construction of a psychomanteum and the results he obtained with individuals who attempted to contact deceased relatives are summarized in his book *Reunions*, and in a paper he wrote for the *Journal of Near-Death Studies* entitled "Family Reunions: Visionary Encounters with the Departed in a Modern-Day Psychomanteum."[454] Psychomanteums were, for many centuries in ancient Greece, places to which people would go to consult with spirits of the deceased. The reports uncovered by Moody confirm that persons who visited these psychomanteums "actually seemed to see and to be in direct communication with the departed during these visits." While many individuals will find it difficult to accept what has been reported about the psychomanteum experience, it is important to keep an open mind and understand that there have been many reports from credible individuals as to their experiences in psychomanteums.

One case worth noting concerns a woman who came to Dr. Moody's psychomanteum with the hope of seeing her late grandfather. She did see and talk to the image of her grandfather, which appeared before her, but unexpectedly, the image emerged from the mirror and comforted her when she began crying upon seeing it.[455] As incredible as these reported experiences are, the reality of the psychomanteum experience has been investigated and confirmed by other researchers. Radin et al. reported:

> After a few minutes to a half-hour in the psycho-manteum, people typically report that the mirror gradually transforms into a window, swirling clouds appear in this window, and then intensely vivid visions are seen through the window. On occasion, visions from the "other side" of the window extend into the psychomanteum itself.[456]

Moody reports that one individual, an editor of a large newspaper, came to his psychomanteum to see if the experience could help her deal with her grief following her son's suicide some months prior. She reported that he appeared to her in the psychomanteum and told her that he was fine and that he loved her.

Moody cites numerous other instances where individuals saw an image in the mirror, although the image was not always the person they had wanted to see. Moody states that "subjects so far have been unanimous in asserting that what took place was completely real."[457] He acknowledges that those who have not had such an experience are quick to believe that the appearances in the psychomanteum are hallucinations.

Moody himself has undergone psychomanteum experiences, and as a psychiatrist and one who has experienced hypnogogia, lucid dreams, and hallucinations following surgery, he adamantly states that "[w]hat I experienced, whatever it was, was in no way related to these other experiences. It was so completely coherent with the reality I have experienced all my life that were I to discount it then so would I be compelled to discount the rest of my life, too, as hallucinatory."[458]

William Roll was an Oxford-educated professor of psychology at the State University of West Georgia when he created a psychomanteum in an attempt to recreate visions of the departed as reported by Moody. Roll reported that nine of the forty-one participants in his study experienced apparitions of deceased loved ones or other "striking reunion experiences."[459]

What exactly happens in the psychomanteum is a mystery. Perhaps it is a projection of the psyche as described by von Franz. Perhaps it is evidence that the world and the forms in it are māyā, or illusion, as described in Mahāyāna Buddhist doctrine.

For example in the Tibetan yoga of the illusory body, the yogin [one who is adept in yoga] is instructed to look

> at that mirrored form with fixity of gaze and mind, and meditating upon it, the figure will come to appear as animated...Visualize it thus as being between the mirror and thyself. Next visualize thine own body as being like that reflected body of the deity; and should the visualization become substantial enough to touch, proceed to visualize any other body thou happenest to see.[460]

Rebirth and Karma

Plato, in a second line of reasoning for the immortality of the soul, argued that reincarnation is true because there are times when we seem to know things that we cannot have learned in this lifetime and must therefore have learned in a prior life. The possibility of reincarnation is not easily dismissed. Even the materialist scientist Carl Sagan acknowledged that the phenomenon deserved more study, as I previously noted. And although the evidence for reincarnation is circumstantial at best, there are numerous accounts of individuals who claim to have lived before and whose stories have been verified by credible scientists. These cases fall into two groups:

- Children who describe a past life when they are very young

- Those who discover a past life when placed under hypnosis

Ian Stevenson was a professor of psychiatry at the University of Virginia for fifty years. During that time he did landmark work investigating evidence for claims of survival from previous incarnations. His work was performed as a serious investigation, under rigorous scientific protocol, of the phenomenon of reincarnation. Stevenson found that children begin to discuss memories of their prior lives at an average age of three and cease discussing them between ages five and seven.[461] The work done by Stevenson was subjected to study by Mills, Haraldsson, and Keil. They investigated cases in five different cultures and found that some children identify themselves with a person whom they have no traditional way of learning about. They concluded that further studies should be undertaken to determine whether memories from a previous life should become a part of the dynamics of child development.[462]

Karma is a frequent topic in discussions on the rebirth phenomenon. While Buddhist traditions vary in their description of the Self, they universally agree on the existence of karma and rebirth. Karma is considered the ultimate example of personal responsibility, for it holds that what happens to individuals is a consequence of their past actions, and that consequence follows them through birth and death. Although Buddhist and Hindu karmic theories share much in common, in some Buddhist sects, karmic theory is caught in a contradiction. In order to explain survival of death and rebirth, Buddhists have to suppose that there is an *atman* [a personal soul], but according to the *anatman* doctrine [no Self], which they accept, there is no such thing.[463] This is just one of many contradictions found in the Buddhist philosophy of death and rebirth. Both existence and nonexistence are affirmed. And both existence and nonexistence are denied. This is illogical, but it is the way of perceiving the reality in Buddhism.[464]

The Self

If there is no Self that is eternal, how is karma able to follow the individual through rebirth? There must be some intangible "mental substance," a Self, which endures from one life to the next. *If* reincarnation is a fact, then what reincarnates must be something like "an egoless I": a Self that survives death, and that carries the seeds of karma from one life to the next. An example of this egoless "I" is described by Emerson in his essay *Nature*, which I described in Chapter 6.

Derek Parfit was a British philosopher who specialized in personal identity and wrote numerous papers and books on the subject. One of his papers argued for the unimportance of identity. Parfit stressed the point that there is a difference between the psychologist's notion of personal identity and that of philosophers. He noted that psychologists are concerned with "what kind of person someone is, or wants to be…But when philosophers discuss the idea of personal identity, it is numerical identity they mean." [465] By numerical, Parfit means "one and the same," not qualitatively identical. He discussed the criteria for deciding if a person yesterday is the same person today, arguing that to be the same person, you have to have the same body today as you had yesterday. He exemplifies this by suggesting that if you were teleported to Mars, you would not be the same person who left Earth, as you do not have bodily continuity. Parfit's paper is an intellectual treatment of personal identity, which argues that we have good philosophical reasons to deny that there is anything such as a Self. [466] Parfit would deny that the men turned into pigs by the witch Circe were not the same men because of their different bodies. I disagree. The pigs exhibited behavior that was recognized as the same behavior the men had exhibited before they were transformed into pigs. To Parfit, it seems, if one receives a heart transplant, they cease to be the same person they were before the transplant because they don't have the same body.

I also disagree with Parfit's dismissal of the idea of an eternal Self. Hane Maung, who also disagrees with Parfit, makes the claim that "consciousness *is* the self…Therefore, since consciousness is the self, the immortality of consciousness is the immortality of the self."[467]

Schopenhauer viewed each mortal as a "pure subject of knowing…this pure subject is what 'remains over as the eternal world eye' after bodily death." Kastrup, whom I discussed previously, concludes, "If Schopenhauer is correct, then we survive our bodily death in the only way that really matters: our felt I-ness persists and probably witnesses the entire dying process."[468] Note the similarity of idea of a "world eye" to the description of the "transparent eyeball" given by Emerson in his *Nature* essay. Kastrup's interpretation of Schopenhauer's philosophy of the Self parallels my argument for an "egoless I" as that which experiences, and that is immortal.

William James identified four traits of the "Self": the material Self; the social Self; the spiritual Self; and the pure Ego.[469] He proceeded to explain what he meant by those terms. There are many definitions of "ego," but the *Dictionary of Psychology*, drawing on the works of Freud, defines it as "It is a largely conscious (1) part of the mind, governed mainly (though not exclusively) by the reality principle, mediating between external reality, the id, and the superego."[470] The "Self," by contrast is what von Franz calls "an inner guiding center, which does not coincide with our consciousness and which can only be further explored through dreams."[471] Does this distinction between "ego" and "Self" answer the question of what survives, and is it in accordance with Buddhist and Hindu theory? Again, I argue in support of the idea of an egoless "I"; think of what survives as a "me," but without conscious memories of a past life. In my view, the Self is simply that which experiences. If regression hypnosis is one day proven to be a valid method of accessing prior lives, then it presumably would be through the process of bringing unconscious memories of prior lives into consciousness.

It is not necessary that one have a continuation of memory in order to be the "same person" from one life to another. In a study of Alzheimer's patients, Psychologist David Ludden asks, "What Remains of the Self after Memory Is Gone?"[472] He notes that late-stage Alzheimer's patients do not experience a loss of Self. Self includes personality, which has shown to persist irrespective of the fact that a person might have no memory of their past life. Ludden found that "consistently across interviews, the researchers found the same pattern when they compared their observations of these patients with their family members' reports. Even when all personal knowledge was gone, personality persisted." If you take away all my memory of who I was and where I came from, there is still a "me," which is experiencing. Total amnesiacs still have a Self that is experiencing, and they continue to have personality traits, which they had before their memory loss.

A Self may be considered to be the "person," the being that unites the physical and psychological components associated with a body from birth to death, and perhaps even in subsequent existences. Chakravarthi Ram-Prasad, distinguished professor of comparative religion and philosophy at Lancaster University, notes that Self can also "mean the 'subject' of awareness,"[473] "a subject of awareness is that *to which* awareness happens…So awareness is awareness of it*self*." This is an important point because I am arguing for the existence of an egoless "I" that experiences, that is a subject of awareness. Wolfgang Fasching puts it this way: "Experiences are not thinkable as being 'ownerless': they are essentially experiences of an experiencing 'I.'"[474]

Ram-Prasad looks to the Buddha's "second sermon" to find what the Buddha thought about a Self. There are basically two arguments put forth by the Buddha against the idea of an *atman* [personal soul]. First, "If this subject-self or *atman* is the 'inner controller,' then it must literally control everything that comes within its purview. But no candidate he can find—for instance, the material body, perception or even awareness—has such control." [475] Secondly, the Buddha argues against the idea of anything existing eternally, unlike the timeless ātman of the Hindu Upanishads. In fact, Ram-Prasad suggests that the Buddha believed that there is something "personal and spiritual" that exists separate and distinct from the body, but that is not eternal.[476] An inept analogy, perhaps wrongly attributed to the Buddha, uses an example of a chariot:

> What makes the chariot what it is?...its yoke, platform, wheels and so on. Take them apart and there is no chariot left. There is no such thing as a chariot in itself; there is no essence to a chariot. Thus it is with a person...when reduced down to these components, she vanishes into nothing.[477]

The above analogy is faulty because if fails to address the fact that a chariot does not "decide" to turn right or left, fall in love, cry, or hate. It is not merely comparing the whole to the sum of the parts. In order to construct a valid analogy, you must include all the parts, and in using a chariot as the subject of the analogy, you are ignoring that "there is something personal and spiritual that exists separate and distinct from the body." Is there something "personal and spiritual," in the words of the Buddha, that exists relative to the chariot? This is where the analogy fails. The arguments against

Hume's bundle theory apply equally to what has been labeled the Buddhist theory of *anatta*, or *no-self*; namely, that it is an attempt to objectivate something which is essentially subjective.[478]

The Buddhist concept of anattā, or no-self, has been referred to as a doctrine holding that nothing exists or that existence is meaningless. Some scholars, however, deny that claim.[479] In contemporary philosophical thinking, Buddhism is considered as advocating a thorough denial of the existence of a Self. This denial of a Self is not, however, universally accepted within Buddhist traditions: "[A] significant minority of Buddhist Indian thinkers reject altogether the *no-self* view, advocating a position according to which the Self exists as a process based on, but not reducible to, the body-mind complex."[480]

The Buddha was frequently queried about topics that bear on the subject of the Self. The questions he was asked are considered "undetermined" because he "did not accept any of the views expressed in the questions." Questions about how the body was related to a permanent "Self/life-principle" could not be answered (so it is said) because he did not accept the idea of a permanent Self. Although he did not embrace a permanent life-principle, he did acknowledge a "changing, empirical life-principle" that a proficient meditator could become aware of as a form of consciousness. Peter Harvey concludes, therefore, that the life-principle is not denied by the Buddha but rather is "accepted, as an invisible phenomena."[481]

Pali Buddhism also holds that "[f]or a life to begin, there must be the coming together, in the womb, of appropriate physical conditions and a flow of *consciousness* from a previous life" (emphasis mine). In some ways, it is problematic to imagine how the "flow of consciousness from a previous life" differs from what is commonly referred to as a Self.

One of the contradictions I see in the doctrinal treatment of consciousness is found in statements by the Dalai Lama: "It's quite clear that consciousness depends on the functioning of the brain, so there is a causal relationship between brain function and the arising of gross consciousness."[482] However, elsewhere he says, "The view that all mental processes are necessary physical processes is a metaphysical assumption, not a scientific fact."[483] This confusion between brain functions and consciousness has been recognized by Alan Wallace, who acknowledges that we can't know if there is a causal relationship between a mind and a body; it may just be that mental and physical processes are highly correlated.[484]

This state of "pure awareness," a state of an egoless "I," allows for something to pass from one lifetime to another. Without the recognition of an egoless "I," it becomes arguably more difficult to deny "nihilism."[485] Rudd echoes my view, where he observes:

> However...it must be that experience in some sense (and blissful experience at that) continues—and that (for the search for *nirvāṇa* to be intelligible as a goal for me to pursue) such experience must still be in some sense *mine*. So the depersonalized witness consciousness cannot be just some other entity; it must still in some sense be me—be already at the heart of what my personal consciousness is, even now.[486]

Unfortunately, Charles Tart and others conflate the terms "ego" and "Self," which I feel underscores the problem with the Buddhist doctrine of no Self. Jung noted that in Eastern philosophy, there is no problem in the idea of a consciousness without an ego,[487] which I argue is essentially an "egoless I." This "I" without the ego is the

Ātman, which is described by Albahari: "the witness—beyond all attributes, beyond action. It can be directly realized as pure consciousness and infinite bliss."[488] Albahari considers the possibility of ownerless consciousness:

> [I]t is worth asking of a chosen Buddhist tradition: What is the most likely relationship between the sense of Self and the ubiquitous feeling of owner-ship (or "mineness") had towards one's thoughts and experiences? Could any form of consciousness survive the possible destruction of these owner-ship feelings? Could ownerless consciousness be an underlying feature of the everyday mind?[489]

Albahari proposes that after the dissolution of a sense of Self, what remains "is a unified perspectival "witness-consciousness" that, insofar as it lacks the illusion of a personal Self, is intrinsically ownerless."[490] Note that she distinguishes between "Self" and "sense of Self." She explains, "The sense of Self is the *appearance* of a Self, pertaining to the reflexive feeling or conscious impression of being a Self."[491] She sets out to construct an argument that there is an unbroken unity of observational witness-consciousness, which is entailed in the state of nirvana as set forth in the sutras.[492]

Huxley commented on this idea of "Self" after ingesting a mind-altering drug:

> [P]ersons are selves and, in one respect at least, I was now a Not-self, simultaneously perceiving and being the Not-self of the things around me. To this new-born Not-self, the behavior, the appearance,

the very thought of the Self it had momentarily ceased to be...seemed not indeed distasteful...but enormously irrelevant.[493]

So what conclusions can be drawn as to the plausibility of continuation of consciousness after the death of the body? As of today, we do not know with certainty what happens when the body dies. Thomas Edison, the American inventor, was curious about what happens when the body dies. In a 1920 interview, Edison told the *Scientific American*:

> I do claim that it is possible to construct an apparatus which will be so delicate that if there are personalities in another existence or sphere who wish to get in touch with us in this existence or sphere, this apparatus will at least give them a better opportunity to express themselves than the tilting tables and raps and Ouija boards and mediums and the other crude methods now purported to be the only means of communication [with the deceased].[494]

Perhaps if Edison had lived long enough to perfect his machine, we would know the answer to Gauguin's final question: Where do we go?

Afterword

I OFTEN THINK OF LIFE as a play like that described in Shakespeare's *As You Like It*. Perhaps we are just actors on a stage, given a script (through our genes and environment), but with just enough free will to make changes to the script as we see fit ("and one man in his time plays many parts"). When the play is over, we depart the stage (life), exiting to wherever. Why does this seem to make sense? Because in near-death experiences, there is a review of one's life—the actions one took in one's life—and the effect those actions had on others. This is much like a review after a stage performance: who dropped their lines, which act was well received, etc.

Perhaps, rather than a play, we are living in a matrix such as that in the film of the same name. As unlikely as that sounds, there are credible scientists and philosophers who argue that it is not only possible, but highly probable.[495]

If the things of our world are the products of a grand design, they may be more integrated and coordinated than we perceive, and perhaps even better (much better!) than we are able to perceive.[496] Gauguin didn't ask the question, "What is our purpose?" but perhaps he should have. Even if we concede that the universe and all that is in it was designed, we are still left with that question unanswered. It seems reasonable to think that the intelligence that designed the universe and everything in it, including us, may have done so to give us the opportunity to experience and learn; this also agrees with reports from those who have had near-death experiences. But it is also possible, to paraphrase William James, that it is the Creator's intention that the purpose of our existence remain baffling; it is left to us to pray and meditate on how to discover what the purpose of our life is and how best to achieve it.

This book seeks to neither prove nor disprove the existence of any particular god, nor the truth or falsity of any particular religion. What this book hopes to do is lend credibility to the idea that an ultimate reality exists behind the doors of perception. It is not important what that reality is called, how one interprets it, or which path to that reality one chooses to follow. What is important is to keep an open mind and keep searching.

I owe a debt of gratitude to all the sources I have drawn on in the creation of this book. I am grateful for the many great thinkers cited in this book who have dared to search for answers that lie outside of the accepted materialist paradigm and for which they have been scorned by their less open-minded peers. In many cases, they risked their livelihoods in order to light the way for the rest of us.

It is my sincere hope that readers of this book will come away with a profound sense of appreciation for the sacred mystery of that ultimate reality that awaits us all.

Bibliography

Albahari, M. (2002). Against no-ātman theories of anattā. *Asian Philosophy, 12*(1), 5–20.

Albahari, M. (2011). Nirvana and ownerless consciousness. In Mark Siderits, Evan Thompson, and Dan Zahavi (Eds.), *Self, No Self* (pp. 79–113). Oxford University Press.

Alexander, E. (2012). *Proof of Heaven: A Neurosurgeon's Journey into the Afterlife.* Simon & Schuster.

Allison, H. E. (1973). Kant's Critique of Berkeley. *Journal of the History of Philosophy, 11*(1), 43–63.

Arnette, J. K. (1997). *An interactionist theory of mind and body* (Doctoral dissertation, Colorado State University).

Atmanspacher, H. (2014). Psychophysical correlations, synchronicity and meaning. *Journal of Analytical Psychology, 59*(2).

Axe, D. (2016). *Undeniable: How Biology Confirms Our Intuition That Life Is Designed*. HarperOne.

Baroetto, G. *After Death*. https://philarchive.org/archive/BARAD-2v3. Accessed May 8, 2020.

Bayne, T., Cleeremans, A., & Wilken, P. (Eds.). (2014). *The Oxford Companion to Consciousness*. Oxford University Press.

Beitman, B. D. (2011). Coincidence studies. *Psychiatric Annals, 41*(12).

Bergson, H. (2010). *Creative Evolution*. Indo-European Publishing.

Besant, A. (1896). *Man and His Bodies* (No. 7). Theosophical Publishing Society.

Betty, S. (2017). *Terminal Lucidity*. https://www.youtube.com/watch?v=uDT3NDwzBpI&t=328s. Accessed January 17, 2020.

Bird, W. R. (1989). *Origin of Species Revisited: Science* (Vols. I & II). Philosophical Library.

Blackmore, S. J. (1982). *Beyond the Body: An Investigation of Out-of-the-Body Experiences*. Academy Chicago Publishers.

Blackmore, S. J. (1984). "A psychological theory of the out-of-body experience." *The Journal of Parapsychology, 48*(3), 201.

Blackmore, S. (1988). A theory of lucid dreams and OBEs. In *Conscious Mind, Sleeping Brain*. Springer.

Blanke, O., & Mohr, C. (2005). "Out-of-body experience, heautoscopy, and autoscopic hallucination of neurological origin: Implications for neurocognitive mechanisms of corporeal awareness and self-consciousness." *Brain Research Reviews*, *50*(1).

Bohlin, H. (1997). *Groundless Knowledge*. Almqvist & Wiksell.

Bohm, D. (1980). *Wholeness and the Implicate Order*. Routledge Classics.

Bohm, D. (1990). "A new theory of the relationship of mind and matter." *Philosophical Psychology*, *3*(2–3), 271–286

Bohm, D. (2004). *Causality and chance in modern physics*. Routledge.

Bonchek, L. I. (2016). "Absence of evidence is not evidence of Absence." *The Journal of Lancaster General Hospital*, *11*(3), 65–66.

Bostrom, N. (2003). "Are we living in a computer simulation?" *The Philosophical Quarterly*, *53*(211), 243–255.

Braithwaite, V. (2010). *Do Fish Feel Pain?* Oxford University Press.

Bulkeley, K., & Bulkeley, P. (2006). *Dreaming beyond Death: A Guide to Pre-Death Dreams and Visions*. Beacon Press.

Bulkeley, K. (Ed.). (2016). *Dreams: A Reader on Religious, Cultural and Psychological Dimensions of Dreaming*. Springer.

Burkhardt, R., & Richard, W. (2011). Lamarck, Cuvier, and Darwin on animal behavior and acquired characters. *The Transformations of Lamarckism.*

Cameron, M. A. (2004). *Synchronicity and Spiritual Development in Alcoholics Anonymous: A Phenomenological Study* (Doctoral dissertation, Saint Louis University).

Campanario, J. M. (2002). "The parallelism between scientists' and students' resistance to new scientific ideas." *International Journal of Science Education*, 24(10).

Capra, F. (2010). *The Tao of Physics: An Exploration of the Parallels between Modern Physics and Eastern Mysticism.* Shambhala Publications.

Cardeña, E. E. and Alvarado, C. S. (2014), pp. 179–180. Anomalous self and identity experiences. In Etzel Cardeña, Steven Jay Lynn, and Stanley Krippner (Eds.), *Varieties of Anomalous Experience* (pp. 17–212). American Psychological Association.

Carr, J. (2003). *The Lives and Theories of Two Great Creative Giants: Carl Jung and David Bohm.* Saybrook Research Institute and Graduate School.

Carroll, S., & Wallace, A. (2017). *The Nature of Reality: A Dialogue Between a Buddhist Scholar and a Theoretical Physicist.*

Cobern, W. W. (2000).The nature of science and the role of knowledge and belief. *Science & Education*, 9(3).

Cockburn, D. (1994). Human beings and giant squids. *Philosophy*, 69(268).

Combs, A., & Holland, M. (1990). *Synchronicity: Science, Myth, and the Trickster*. Paragon House Publishers.

Cooper, J. M., & Hutchinson, D. S. (Eds.). (1997). *Plato: Complete Works, Vol. I–IV*. Hackett Publishing.

Cooper, P. D. (2017). "A real fifth dimension?" *Explore: The Journal of Science and Healing, 13*(1).

Corbett, L. (2019). *Psyche and the Sacred: Spirituality beyond Religion*. Routledge.

Cremo, M. A. (2003). *Human Devolution A Vedic Alternative to Darwin's Theory*. Torchlight Publishing.

Crick, F. (1994). *The Astonishing Hypothesis*. Scribners.

Darwin, C. (1872). *On the Origin of Species by Means of Natural Selection*. Easton Press.

Darwin, C. (1892). *The formation of vegetable mould through the action of worms: with observations on their habits* (Vol. 37). Appleton.

Davies, P. (1992). *The Mind of God: Science and the Search for Ultimate Meaning*. Simon and Schuster.

Dawkins, R. (1986). *The Blind Watchmaker*. Penguin Books Ltd.

Dawkins, R. (1996). *The Blind Watchmaker: Why the Evidence of Evolution Reveals a Universe without Design*. W. W. Norton & Company.

Deguchi, Y., Garfield, J. L., & Priest, G. (2008). The way of the dialetheist: Contradictions in Buddhism. *Philosophy East and West, 58*(3), 395–402.

Dennett, D. C. (1991). *Consciousness Explained*. Back Bay Books.

De Waal, F. B. (2012). The antiquity of empathy. *Science, 336*(6083), 874–876.

Diaconis, P., & Mosteller, F. "Methods for Studying Coincidences," *Journal of the American Statistical Association*, 84(408).

Dillon, J. (Ed.). (1991). *The Enneads*. Penguin UK.

Dossey, L., Greyson, B., Sturrock, P. A., & Tucker, J. B. (2011). "Consciousness—What Is It?" *Journal of Cosmology, 14.*

Dreyfus, G. (2011). Self and subjectivity: A middle way approach, in Siderits, M., Thompson, E., & Zahavi, D. (Eds.) *Self, no self?: Perspectives from analytical, phenomenological, and Indian traditions*. Oxford University Press.

Dunlap, K. (1914). "The self and the ego." *Psychological Review*, 21(1), 62.

Easwaran, E. (2007). *The Upanishads*. Nilgiri Press.

Eden, M. (1967). Inadequacies of neo-Darwinian evolution as a scientific theory. In *The Wistar Institute Symposium Monograph*, 5, 5–19.

Edgcombe, D. (2003). *Beyond the Physical: An Exploration into the Structure of Reality through One Individual's Exceptional Experiences.* (Master's Dissertation, Institute of Transpersonal Psychology).

Edinger, E. F. (1984). *The Mystery of the Coniunctio.* Inner City Books.

Edrington, D. *A Palliative for Wandering Attention.* Edrington quotes Watson. http://www.rebprotocol.net/hemisyncandphasing.pdf. Accessed July 1, 2020.

Elster, J. (1983). *Sour Grapes: Studies in the Subversion of Rationality.* Cambridge University Press.

Emerson, R. W. (1983). *Essays and Lectures.* Library of America 15.

Evans-Wentz, W. Y. (1958). *Tibetan Yoga and Secret Doctrines.* Oxford University Press.

Evans-Wentz, W. Y. (1960). *The Tibetan Book of the Dead.* Oxford University Press.

Evans-Wentz, W. Y. (1968). *The Tibetan Book of the Great Liberation.* Oxford University Press.

Facco, E., Agrillo, C., & Greyson, B. (2015). Epistemological implications of near-death experiences and other non-ordinary mental expressions: Moving beyond the concept of altered state of consciousness. *Medical Hypotheses*, *85*(1).

Faraday, A. (1976). *The Dream Game*. HarperCollins Publishers.

Fasching, W. (2011). Phenomenological Reflections on the Indian Notion of Witness-Consciousness. *Self, No Self?: Perspectives from Analytical, Phenomenological, and Indian Traditions*.

Fechner, G. T., & Lowrie, W. (1947). *Religion of a Scientist*. Pantheon Books.

Fechner, G. T. (2005). *The Little Book of Life After Death*. Red Wheel/Weiser, LLC.

Festinger, L. (1957). *A Theory of Cognitive Dissonance*. Stanford University Press.

Feynman, R. P. (2006). *QED: The Strange Theory of Light and Matter*. Princeton University Press.

Fodor, J., & Piattelli-Palmarini, M. (2011). *What Darwin Got Wrong*. Profile books.

Foster, J. B. (1964). Evolution of mammals on islands. *Nature*, *202*(4929).

Foster, R. D. (2010). *Effects of a near-death experience learning module on grief*. University of North Texas.

Gagliano, M., Renton, M., Depczynski, M., & Mancuso, S. (2014). Experience teaches plants to learn faster and forget slower in environments where it matters. *Oecologia, 175*(1), 63–72.

Garcia-Romeu, A. P., & Tart, C. T. (2013). Altered states of consciousness and transpersonal psychology. In Harris L. Friedman and Glenn Hartelius (Eds.), *The Wiley-Blackwell Handbook of Transpersonal Psychology* (pp. 121–140). John Wiley & Sons, Ltd.

Geison, Gerald 1996. *The Notebooks of Louis Pasteur.* Princeton University Press.

Godfrey-Smith, P. (2016). *Other minds: The Octopus, the Sea, and the Deep Origins of Consciousness.* Farrar, Straus, and Giroux.

Goswami, A. (1995). *The Self-Aware Universe: How Consciousness Creates the Material World.* Penguin.

Greyson, B. (2010). Implications of near-death experiences for a postmaterialist psychology. *Psychology of Religion and Spirituality*, 2(1), 41.

Gribbin, J. (1984). *In Search of Schrödinger's Cat: Quantum Physics and Reality.* Bantam.

Grof, S. (1983). East and West: Ancient wisdom and modern science. *Journal of Transpersonal Psychology, 15*(1).

Gopnik, A., & Griffiths, T. (2017). What Happens to Creativity as We Age?

https://www.nytimes.com/2017/08/19/opinion/sunday/what-happens-to-creativity-as-we-age.html.

Goswami, A. (1995). *The Self-Aware Universe: How Consciousness Creates The Material World.* Penguin.

Green, C. E., & McCreery, C. (1975). *Apparitions.* Institute of Psychophysical Research, Oxford.

Greyson, B. (2010). Implications of near-death experiences for a postmaterialist psychology. *Psychology of Religion and Spirituality, 2*(1).

Haldane, J. B. S. (2002). *Possible Worlds.* Transaction Publishers.

Heisenberg, W., & Bond, B. (1958). *Physics and Philosophy: The Revolution in Modern Science.* HarperCollins Publishers, Inc.

Harvey, P. (1993). The mind body relationship in Pāli Buddhism: A philosophical investigation. *Asian Philosophy, 3*(1), 29–41.

Ho, D. Y. (1995). Selfhood and Identity in Confucianism, Taoism, Buddhism, and Hinduism: Contrasts with the West. *Journal for the Theory of Social Behaviour, 25*(2), 115–139.

Hoffman, D. (2019). *The Case Against Reality: Why Evolution Hid the Truth from Our Eyes.* W. W. Norton & Company.

Holden, J. M. (2009). *Veridical perception in near-death experiences.* In J. M. Holden, B. Greyson, & D. James (Eds.), *The handbook of near-death experiences: Thirty years of investigation* (p. 185–211). Praeger/ABC-CLIO. Holden.

Holden, J. M., & Hagan III, J. C., (Eds.) (2017). The science of near-death experiences. *Missouri Medicine.*

Homer. *The Iliad and the Odyssey.* Reprinted by Barnes & Noble, Inc., Book X.

Honderich, T. (1995), *The Oxford Companion to Philosophy.* Oxford University Press.

Hudson, T. J. (1902). *The Law of Psychic Phenomena.* AC McClurg & Company.

Huxley, A. (1990). *The Doors of Perception.* Harper Collins Publishers, Inc.

Irwin, L. (2015). Mystical Knowledge and Near-Death Experience. In *Death, Dying, and Mysticism* (pp. 153–175). Palgrave Macmillan, New York.

Jacob, F. (1977). "Evolution and tinkering." *Science*, 196(4295).

Jacobi, J. (1971). *Complex/archetype/symbol in the psychology of CG Jung* (Vol. 57). Princeton University Press.

Jaffé, A. (1979). *Apparitions: An Archetypal Approach to Death Dreams and Ghosts* (No. 1). Spring Publications.

James, W. (1890). *The Principles of Psychology*, Volumes One and Two. Dover Publications, Inc.

James, W. (1987). *Writings 1902–1910*. The Library of America.

Jennings, H. S. (1906). *Behavior of the Lower Organisms* (No. 10). Columbia University Press.

Jonas, H. (1986). Parallelism and Complementarity: The Psycho-Physical Problem in Spinoza and in the Succession of Niels Bohr. In *Spinoza and the Sciences*. Springer.

Jung, C. G. (1953). *Psychology and Alchemy*. Princeton University Publishing.

Jung, C. G. (1959). *The Archetypes and the Collective Unconscious*, Trans. RFC Hull. Princeton University Publishing.

Jung, C. G. (1960). *The Structure and Dynamics of the Psyche*. Collected works: Vol. 8. Trans. R. F. C. Hull. Princeton University Press.

Jung, C. G., & Jaffé, Aniela. (1963). *Memories, Dreams, Reflections* (Vol. 268). Vintage.

Kafatos, M., Tanzi, R. E., & Chopra, D. (2011). How consciousness becomes the physical universe. *Journal of Cosmology*, 14.

Kastrup, B. (2014). *Why Materialism Is Baloney: How True Skeptics Know There Is No Death and Fathom Answers to Life, the Universe, and Everything*. Iff Books.

Kastrup, B. (2019). "Reasonable inferences from quantum mechanics: A response to quantum misuse in psychic literature." *Journal of Near-Death Studies*, 37(3).

Kastrup, B. (2020). *Schopenhauer's Sense of Self.*

https://iai.tv/articles/schopenhauers-sense-of-self-auid-1329. Accessed May 3, 2020.

Keutzer, C. S. (1983). The Theory of "Formative Causation" and its Implications for Archetypes, Parallel Inventions, and the "Hundredth Monkey Phenomenon." *The Journal of Mind and Behavior*, 353–367.

Kuijsten, M. (2009). Close-mindedness and mysticism in science: Commentary on John Smythies's review of reflections on the dawn of consciousness. *The Jaynesian*, 3.

Kjellgren, A., Lyden, F., & Norlander, T. (2008). Sensory isolation in flotation tanks: altered states of consciousness and effects on well-being. *The Qualitative Report*, 13(4), 636–656.

Koch, C. (2014). Ubiquitous Minds. *Scientific American Mind*, 25(1), 26–29.

Koch, C. (2014). "Is consciousness universal." *Scientific American Mind*, 25.

Koestler, A. (1967). *The Ghost in the Machine*. Hutchinson.

Koestler, A. (1972). *The Roots of Coincidence*. Random House.

Koonin, E. V., & Wolf, Y. I. (2009). "Is evolution Darwinian or/and Lamarckian?" *Biology Direct*, 4(1).

Krippner, S., & Faith, L. (2001). "Exotic dreams: A cross-cultural study." *Dreaming*, 11(2), 73–82.

Krishnamurti, J., & Rajagopal, D. (1989). *Think on These Things*. HarperPerennial.

Kuhn, T. S. (2012). *The Structure of Scientific Revolutions*. University of Chicago Press.

Kumar, M. (2008). *Quantum: Einstein, Bohr, and the Great Debate about the Nature of Reality*. W. W. Norton & Company.

Kurtz, P. (1986). *The Transcendental Temptation: A Critique of Religion and the Paranormal*. Prometheus Books.

Kutschera, U. (2003). A comparative analysis of the Darwin-Wallace papers and the development of the concept of natural selection. *Theory in Biosciences*, 122(4).

LaBerge, Stephen (1985). *Lucid Dreaming*. Jeremy P. Tarcher, Inc.

Lama, D. (2002). *Sleeping, Dreaming, and Dying: An Exploration of Consciousness*. Simon and Schuster.

Lama, D. (2005). *The Universe in a Single Atom: The Convergence of Science and Spirituality.* Harmony.

Laszlo, E. (2004), *Science and the Akashic Field.* Inner Traditions.

Laszlo, E. (2016). *What Is Reality?: The New Map of Cosmos, Consciousness, and Existence.* SelectBooks, Inc.

Laval, R. (2013). *Making Sense of Synchronicity* (Doctoral dissertation, University of Northern British Columbia).

Lennox, J. G. (1993). "Darwin was a teleologist." *Biology and Philosophy*, *8*(4).

Lescarboura, A. C. (1920). "Edison's views on life and death." *Scientific American*, 123(18), 446–460.

Leuba, J. H. (1915). "William James and immortality." *The Journal of Philosophy, Psychology and Scientific Methods*, 12(15), 409–416.

Lewin, R. (1980). "Is your brain really necessary?" *Science, New Series*, 2010(4475).

Lewis, M., & Spignesi, S. J. (2009). *100 Best Beatles Songs: A Passionate Fan's Guide.* Hachette UK.

Libet, B. (2004). *Mind Time: The Temporal Factor in Consciousness.* Harvard University Press.

Lindsay, W. L. (1876). "Mind in plants." *Journal of Mental Science*, *21*(96).

Loftus, E. F. (1997). "Creating false memories." *Scientific American*, 277(3), 70–75.

Loftus, E. F. (1980). *Memory*. Addison-Wesley Publishing Company.

Long, A. (1995). "A response to David Cockburn." *Philosophy*, 70(271).

Losch, A. (Ed.). (2017). *What Is Life? On Earth and Beyond*. Cambridge University Press.

Ludwig, A. M. (1966). "Altered states of consciousness." *Archives of general Psychiatry*, 15(3).

Lynn, S. J., Fassler, O., & Knox, J. (2005). Hypnosis and the altered state debate: something more or nothing more? *Contemporary Hypnosis*, 22(1), 39–45.

MacDonald, G. F., Cove, J. L., Laughlin Jr, C. D., & McManus, J. (1989). Mirrors, portals, and multiple realities. *Zygon®*, 24(1), 39–64.

Maddox, J. (1981). A book for burning. *Nature*, *293*(5830), 245–246.

Mancuso, S. (2018). *The Revolutionary Genius of Plants: A New Understanding of Plant Intelligence and Behavior*. Simon and Schuster.

Mansfield, p. 46. See Storm, L. (1999). "Synchronicity, causality, and acausality." *Journal of Parapsychology, 63*(3).

Marais, E. (2009). *The Soul of the White Ant.* A Distant Mirror.

Maung, H. H. (2007). *Consciousness: An Enquiry into the Metaphysics of the Self.* Lulu Press.

Mayr, E. (1988). *Toward a New Philosophy of Biology: Observations of an Evolutionist* (No. 211). Harvard University Press.

McFadden, J. (2002). *Quantum Evolution.* W. W. Norton & Company.

Meyer, S. C. (2013). *Darwin's Doubt: The Explosive Origin of Animal Life and the Case for Intelligent Design.* HarperOne.

Miller, A. I. (2010). *137: Jung, Pauli, and the Pursuit of a Scientific Obsession.* W. W. Norton & Company.

Mills, A., Haraldsson, E., & Keil, H. J. (1994). "Replication studies of cases suggestive of reincarnation by three independent investigators." *Journal of the American Society for Psychical Research,* 88(3), 207–219.

Milton, Richard (1992). *Shattering the Myths of Darwinism.* CreateSpace.

Milton, R. (1996). *Alternative Science: Challenging the Myths of the Scientific Establishment.* Inner Traditions/Bear & Co.

Miralles, A., Raymond, M., & Lecointre, G. (2019). "Empathy and compassion toward other species decrease with evolutionary divergence time." *Scientific Reports*, 9(1), 1–8.

Moncrieff, M. M. (1951). *The Clairvoyant Theory of Perception: A New Theory of Vision*. Faber and Faber Limited.

Moody, R. A. (1975). *Life after Life*. Bantam Books.

Moody, R. A. (1992). "Family reunions: Visionary encounters with the departed in a modern-day psychomanteum." *Journal of Near-Death Studies*, 11(2), 83–121.

Moody, R. A. (1992b). *Coming Back: A Psychiatrist Explores Past-Life Journeys*. Bantam.

Moody, R. A., & Perry, P. (1995). *Reunions: Visionary Encounters with Departed Loved Ones*. Ivy Books.

Morse, M., & Perry, P. (1991). *Closer to the Light*. Random House Digital, Inc.

Nagel, A. H. (1997). "Are plants conscious?" *Journal of Consciousness Studies*, 4(3).

Neale, M. (2009). *Mindfulness Meditation: An Integration of Perspectives from Buddhism, Science and Clinical Psychology* (Doctoral dissertation).

Nechita, Elena. (2010). "Some considerations on seriality and synchronicity." *BRAIN. Broad Research in Artificial Intelligence and Neuroscience*, 1(1).

Newton, M. (2010). *Journey of Souls: Case Studies of Life between Lives*. Llewellyn Worldwide.

Noll, R. (1997). *The Jung Cult: The Origins of a Charismatic Movement*. Simon and Schuster.

Otto, R. (1958). *The Idea of the Holy* (Vol. 14). Oxford University Press.

Pailthorp, C. (1969). Knowledge as justified, true belief. *The Review of Metaphysics*, 23(1).

Palmieri, A., Calvo, V., Kleinbub, J. R., Meconi, F., Marangoni, M., Barilaro, P., & Sessa, P. (2014). "'Reality' of near-death-experience memories: evidence from a psychodynamic and electrophysiological integrated study." *Frontiers in Human Neuroscience, 8*.

Parfit, D. (1995). *The Unimportance of Identity*. In *The Oxford Handbook of the Self*.

Parrish, D. (2006). *Nothing I See Means Anything: Quantum Questions, Quantum Answers*. Sentient Publications.

Pearsall, P., Schwartz, G. E., & Russek, L. G. (2000). "Changes in heart transplant recipients that parallel the personalities of their donors." *Integrative Medicine*, 2(2–3).

Peat, F. D. (1987). *Synchronicity: The Bridge Between Matter and Mind.* Bantam.

Penfield, W. (1975). *Mystery of the Mind: A Critical Study of Consciousness and the Human Brain.* Princeton University Press.

Perez-De-Albeniz, A., & Holmes, J. (2000). "Meditation: Concepts, effects and uses in therapy." *International Journal of Psychotherapy,* 5(1).

Phipps, Carter. (2000). "No escape for the ego: An interview with venerable master Sheng-yen." *Lenox* 17, 50.

Pinto, Y., Neville, D. A., Otten, M., Corballis, P. M., Lamme, V. A., et al. (2017). "Split brain: Divided perception but undivided consciousness." *Brain,* 140(5), 1231–1237.

Planck, M. (1949). *Scientific Autobiography.* F. Gaynor, trans. New York: Philosophical Library.

Planck, M. (1959). *The New Science.* Meridian Books.

Pollan, M. (2019). *How to Change Your Mind: What the New Science of Psychedelics Teaches Us about Consciousness, Dying, Addiction, Depression, and Transcendence.* Penguin Books.

Ponte, D. V., & Schäfer, L. (2013). "Carl Gustav Jung, quantum physics and spiritual mind: A mystical vision of the twenty-first century." *Behavioral Sciences,* 3.

Potts, M. (2012). "Does N, N-dimethyltryptamine (DMT) adequately explain near-death experiences?" *Journal of Near-Death Studies*, 31(1).

Progoff, I. (1973). *Jung, Synchronicity, and Human Destiny: Noncausal Dimensions of Human Experience.* Dell Publishing Co., Inc.

Pyun, Y. D. (2015). "Creating past-life identity in hypnotic regression." *International Journal of Clinical and Experimental Hypnosis*, 63(3), 365–372.

Radin, D. I., & Rebman, J. M. (1996). Are phantasms fact or fantasy? A preliminary investigation of apparitions evoked in the laboratory. *JOURNAL-SOCIETY FOR PSYCHICAL RESEARCH, 61,* 65–87. *Research.*

Radin, Dean. (1997). *The Conscious Universe: The Scientific Truth of Psychic Phenomena.* HarperOne.

Radin, D. (2006). *Entangled Minds: Extrasensory Experiences in a Quantum Reality.* Pocket Books.

Radin, D. (2018). *Real Magic: Ancient Wisdom, Modern Science, and a Guide to the Secret Power of the Universe.* Harmony.

Ramachandran, V. S., & Hirstein, W. (1998). "The perception of phantom limbs. The DO Hebb lecture." *Brain: A Journal of Neurology,* 121(9).

Ring, K., & Cooper, S. (2008). *Mindsight: Near-Death and Out-Of-Body Experiences in the Blind.* iUniverse.

Rinpoche, S. (1990). *What Survives?* The teachings of Tibetan Buddhism.

Riverside Publishing Company. (1984). *Webster's II New Riverside University Dictionary*. Riverside.

Roll, W. G. (2004). "Psychomanteum research: A pilot study." *Journal of Near-Death Studies*.

Roob, Alexander. (2006). *Alchemy and Mysticism*. Taschen.

Rosenblum, B., & Kuttner, F. (2011). *Quantum Enigma: Physics Encounters Consciousness*. Oxford University Press.

Rousseau, D., & Eng., B. (2011). "Near-death experiences and the mind-body relationship: a systems-theoretical perspective." *Journal of Near-Death Studies*, 29(3).

Rudd, A. (2015). "No self? Some reflections on Buddhist theories of personal identity." *Philosophy East and West*, 65(3), 869–891.

Russell, B. (1912, January). On the notion of cause. In *Proceedings of the Aristotelian Society* (Vol. 13). Aristotelian Society, Wiley.

Russell, B. (1945). *A History of Western Philosophy*. Simon & Schuster.

Russell, B. (2000). *The Autobiography of Bertrand Russell: 1872–1914. (Vol. 1)*. Little, Brown.

Sabom, M. B. (1998). *Light and Death: One Doctor's Fascinating Account of Near-Death Experiences*. Zondervan.

Sabom, M. B. (1982). *Recollections of Death: A Medical Investigation.* Harper & Row.

Sagan, C. (1977). *The Dragons of Eden.* Random House.

Sagan, C. (1996). *The Demon Haunted World.* Random House.

Schmicker, M. (2000). *Best Evidence.* Writers Club Press.

Schopenhauer, A. (1966). *The World as Will and Representation.* Dover Publications, Inc.

Schopenhauer, A. (1970). *Essays and Aphorisms* (Vol. 227). Penguin UK.

Schwenn, H. (2014). *Out-of-Body Experiences: An Exploration of the Phenomenological Features and the Long-Term Aftereffects* (Doctoral dissertation, Institute of Transpersonal Psychology).

Schwerin, A. (2007). "Hume and the self: A critical response." *Journal of Scottish Philosophy*, 5(1).

Searle, J. R. (1992). *The Rediscovery of the Mind.* MIT press.

Shlain, L. (1993). *Art & Physics.* Quill.

Sheldrake, A. R. (1980). "Three approaches to biology. 1. The mechanistic theory of life." *Theoria to Theory*, 14.

Sheldrake, R. (1987). "Part I: Mind, memory, and archetype morphic resonance and the collective unconscious." *Psychological Perspectives.*

Sheldrake, R. (2003). *The Sense of Being Stared At: And Other Aspects of the Extended Mind*. Random House.

Sheldrake, R. (2006). "Morphic fields." *World Futures*.

Sheldrake, R. (2012). *Science Set Free: 10 Paths to New Discovery*. Deepak Chopra.

Sheldrake, R. (2011). *Dogs that Know When Their Owners Are Coming Home: And Other Unexplained Powers of Animals*. Three Rivers Press.

Sheldrake, R. (2011). *The Presence of the Past: Morphic Resonance and the Habits of Nature*. Icon Books Ltd.

Shermer, M. (1997). *Why People Believe Weird Things: Pseudoscience, Superstition, and Bogus Notions of Our Time*. Henry Holt and Company LLC.

Shin, K. (2013). *The Concept of Self and Its Implication for Salvation in Hinduism, Buddhism, and Christianity*. Drew University.

Singer, J. (1984). Reviewed works: Wholeness and the implicate order by David Bohm. *San Francisco Jung Institute Library Journal*, 4(4).

Skrbina, D. (2017). *Panpsychism in the West*. MIT Press.

Smith, H. (1991). *The World's Religions*. HarperOne.

Smith, H. (1992). *Forgotten Truth*. HarperCollins.

Smith, H. (2000). *Cleansing the Doors of Perception: The Religious Significance of Entheogenic Plants and Chemicals*. Tarcher, Putnam.

Sneddon, L. U. (2006). "Ethics and welfare: Pain perception in fish." *Bulletin of the European Association of Fish Pathologists*, 26(1).

Stapp, H. P. (1996). "The hard problem: A quantum approach." *Journal of Consciousness Studies*, 3(3), 194–210.

Stapp, H. P. (2011). *Mindful Universe: Quantum Mechanics and the Participating Observer*. Springer Science & Business Media.

Steiner, R. (2014). *Unifying Humanity Spiritually: Through the Christ Impulse* (Vol. 165). Rudolf Steiner Press.

Storm, L. (1999). "Synchronicity, causality, and acausality." *Journal of Parapsychology*, 63(3), 247–270.

Strassman, R. (2000). *DMT: The Spirit Molecule: A Doctor's Revolutionary Research into the Biology of Near-Death And Mystical Experiences*. Simon and Schuster.

Szyf, M. (2014). "Lamarck revisited: epigenetic inheritance of ancestral odor fear conditioning." *Nature Neuroscience*, 17(1).

Talbot, M. (1991). *The Holographic Universe*. HarperCollins.

Taylor, G. R. (1983). *The Great Evolution Mystery*. Harper & Row Publishers, Inc.

Taylor, J. *Where People Fly and Water Runs Uphill*. Warner Books.

Teasdale, W. (2001). *The Mystic Heart: Discovering a Universal Spirituality in the World's Religions*. New World Library.

Theise, N. D., & Kafatos, M. (2013). "Sentience everywhere: complexity theory, panpsychism & the role of sentience in self-organization of the universe." *Journal of Consciousness Exploration & Research*, 4(4).

Tietze, T. R. Some perspectives on survival, in White, J. W. (1974). *Frontiers of Consciousness: The Meeting Ground between Inner and Outer Reality*. The Julian Press, Inc.

Tompkins, P., & Bird, C. (1973). *The Secret Life of Plants* (No. QK50. T65I 1973.). Harper & Row.

Tompkins, P. (1997). *The Secret Life of Nature: Living in Harmony with the Hidden World of Nature Spirits from Fairies to Quarks*. Harper San Francisco.

Trewavas A. J., & Baluška F. (2011). *The Ubiquity of Consciousness: The Ubiquity of Consciousness, Cognition and Intelligence in Life*. EMBO Rep.

Vaitl, D., Birbaumer, N., Gruzelier, J., Jamieson, G. A., Kotchoubey, B., Kübler, A., & Sammer, G. (2005). "Psychobiology of altered states of consciousness." *Psychological Bulletin*, 131(1), 98.

Vallee, J., & Strieber, W. (1988). *Dimensions: A Casebook of Alien Contact*. Contemporary Books.

Van der Sluijs, M. (2009). Three ancient reports of near-death experiences: Bremmer revisited. *Journal of Near-Death Studies*, 27(4), 223.

Van Lommel, P. (2011). "Near death experiences: the experience of the self as real and not as an illusion." *Annals of the New York Academy of Sciences*, 1234(1).

Vardamis, A. A., & Owens, J. E. (1999). Ernest Hemingway and the Near-Death Experience. *Journal of Medical Humanities*, 20(3), 203–217.

Von Franz, M. L. (1980). *Alchemy: An Introduction to the Symbolism and the Psychology* (Vol. 5). Inner City Books.

Von Franz, M. L. (1998). *On Dreams and Death*. Open Court.

Von Franz, M. L. (1998). *Dreams: A Study of the Dreams of Jung, Descartes, Socrates, and Other Historical Figures*. Shambhala Publications.

Von Franz, M. L. (1999). *Archetypal Dimensions of the Psyche*. Shambhala Publications.

Von Franz, M. L. (2001). *Psyche and Matter*. Shambhala Publications.

Voss, U., Holzmann, R., Tuin, I., & Hobson, A. J. (2009). "Lucid dreaming: A state of consciousness with features of both waking and non-lucid dreaming." *Sleep*, 32(9).

Webb, M. (2017). "Religious experience," *The Stanford Encyclopedia of Philosophy* (Winter 2017 Edition), E. N. Zalta (ed.), https://plato.stanford.edu/archives/win2017/entries/religious-experience/.

Webster, B. (1983). "The plant biologists turn over a new leaf." *New York Times.*

White, J. W. (1974). *Frontiers of Consciousness: The Meeting Ground between Inner and Outer Reality.* The Julian Press.

Whitton, J. L., & Fisher, J. (1986). *Life between Life: Scientific Explorations into the Void Separating One Incarnation from the Next.* Doubleday Books.

Wigner, E. P. (1970). "Physics and the explanation of life." *Foundations of Physics*, 1(1).

Wilhelm, R., Trans. (1967). *I Ching or Book of Changes.* Bollingen Series 19.

Wilhelm, H. (Ed.). (2011). *The I Ching or Book of Changes* (Vol. 170). Princeton University Press.

Wilson, C. (1987). *Afterlife: An Investigation.* Doubleday.

Wilson, C. (1988). *Beyond the Occult.* Carroll & Graff Publishers, Inc.

Woerlee, G. M. (2011). "Could Pam Reynolds hear? A new investigation into the possibility of hearing during this famous near-death experience." *Journal of Near-Death Studies*, 30(1).

Wolf, A. F. (1994). *The Dreaming Universe: Investigations of the Middle Realm of Consciousness and Matter.* Simon & Schuster.

Woodhouse, M. B. (1994). "Out-of-body experiences and the mind-body problem." *New Ideas in Psychology*, 12(1), 1–16.

Woolley, B. (2002). *The Queen's Conjurer: The Science and Magic of Dr. John Dee, Advisor to Queen Elizabeth I.* Macmillan.

Wulf, D. M. (2014). Mystical experiences. In Etzel Cardeña, Steven Jay Lynn, and Stanley Krippner (Eds.), *Varieties of Anomalous Experience* (pp. 369–408). American Psychological Association.

Zajonc, A. (1995). *Catching the Light: The Entwined History of Light and Mind.* Oxford University Press.

Zaleski, C. (1988). *Otherworld Journeys: Accounts of Near-Death Experience in Medieval and Modern Times.* Oxford University Press.

Zukov, G. (1979). *The Dancing Wu Li Masters.* William Morrow and Company.

Notes

1 https://en.wikipedia.org/wiki/Where_Do_We_Come_From%3F_What_Are_We%3F_Where_Are_We_Going%3F. Accessed Feb. 2, 2020.

2 https://www.mortylefkoe.com/how-our-language-determines-our-reality/. Accessed 12/30/2019.

3 Kuijsten, M. (2009). Close-mindedness and mysticism in science: Commentary on John Smythies's review of reflections on the dawn of consciousness. *The Jaynesian, 3*, pp. 1–9; Corbett, L. (2019). *Psyche and the sacred: Spirituality beyond religion*. Routledge. Corbett notes "'real' does not have to mean 'provable by observation of the five senses.' Many experiences that science cannot explain—such as falling in love—are important emotionally and it would be absurd to dismiss them as not real just because they cannot be demonstrated rigorously by the scientific method."

4 Huxley, A. (2009), p. 8.

5 Corbett, L. (2019), p. 4. Corbett argues that this experience of the sacred "leads to *knowledge* that there is a transcendent reality, rather than mere *belief* in it." Other means of accessing the transcendent reality include certain dance rituals practiced by indigenous peoples.

6 LaBerge, Stephen (1985). *Lucid Dreaming*. Jeremy P. Tarcher, Inc., p. 228.

7 Festinger, Leon (1957).

8 Riverside Publishing Company. (1984). *Webster's II new Riverside university dictionary*. Riverside Pub. Co.

9 See my discussion of the work of Rupert Sheldrake in Chapter 2.

10 Honderich, Ted. (1995), *The Oxford Companion to Philosophy*. Oxford University Press, p. 842.

11 Shermer, M. (1997), p. vi.

12 James, William. (1890), p. 284.

13 Bohlin, Henrik. (1997). *Groundless Knowledge*. Almqvist & Wiksell, p. 79.

14 Krishnamurti, J., & Rajagopal, D. (1989), pp. 68–69.

15 Festinger (1957).

16 Milton, R. (1996), p. 108, quoting Festinger, Leon (1957).

17 Elster, Jon. (1983), p. 123. In his book, Elster uses as an example the case where someone, on failing to get a promotion, argues that his superiors fear his ability.

18 Kuhn, T. S. (2012). *The structure of scientific revolutions*. University of Chicago Press, p. 59.

19 Schopenhauer, A. (1970). Schopenhauer stated: "It is quite natural that we should adopt a defensive and negative attitude towards every new opinion concerning something on which we have already an opinion of our own." While it may be "quite natural," he also notes that a new idea "demands renewed efforts of us and declares our former efforts to have been in vain." It is no wonder new ideas receive such ridicule.

20 Elster, Jon (1983).

21 Pailthorp, C. (1969). Knowledge as justified, true belief. *The Review of Metaphysics*, *23*(1), 25–47.

22 Russell, Bertrand (1945), p. 823.

23 Cobern, William W. (2000), pp. 219–246.

24 Progoff, I. (1973), p. 51.

25 Planck, M. (1949). Planck's quote is also found in: Barber, Bernard. (1961), Resistance by Scientists to Scientific Discovery, in *Science, New Series*, Vol. 34, No. 3479, p. 597.

26 Campanario, Juan Miguel. (2002), p. 1100.

27 Kuhn, T. S. (1962).

28 Koestler, Arthur. (1972), p. 19; Kuhn, T. S. (1962).

29 Laszlo, E. (2016), p.137–38; Sagan, Carl (1977), p. 7.

30 Laszlo, E. (2016), p. 137; Sagan, Carl (1996), p. 302.

31 Campanario, J. M. (2002), pp. 1095–1110.

32 Milton, Richard (1992), p. 216. Milton is quoting from Geison, Gerald 1996. *The Notebooks of Louis Pasteur*. Princeton University Press.

33 Von Franz, M. L. (1980), pp. 175–176.

34 Festinger, Leon (1957), p. 269.

35 Russell, Bertrand. (1945), p. 823.

36 Gopnik, Alison and Tom Griffiths. https://www.nytimes.com/2017/08/19/opinion/sunday/what-happens-to-creativity-as-we-age.html. Accessed July 5, 2019.

37 Corbett, L. (2019), p. 26.

38 In a recorded interview, Carl Jung had this to say about belief: "Belief is a difficult thing for me. I don't believe. I must have a reason for a certain hypothesis. Either I know a thing and then I know it. I don't need to believe it."

39 Sheldrake, R. (2013), p. 265.

40 Radin, D. (2018), p. 75. Now in my seventy-sixth year, I can attest to the fact that although I haven't had an epiphany or a gratuitous experience of the sacred, I am blessed to have deep faith. This has come about through a profound appreciation of the beauty of the natural world, a feeling of deep love for those who share my life, and a habit of expressing gratitude daily; I have slipped into a comfortable state of mind where I am watching joyfully and fearlessly as the remainder of my life unfolds.

41 Talbot, M. (1991), pp. 90–91.

42 Talbot, M. (1991), p. 96.

43 Talbot, M. (1991), p. 91.

44 Huxley, A. (1990), p. 79.

45 Wigner, E. P. (1970). Physics and the explanation of life. *Foundations of Physics, 1*(1), 35–45. Wigner states: "If no solid knowledge is available in a field, it is good if representatives of neighbor sciences put forward the views which appear most natural from their own vantage point." Wigner received the Nobel Prize in physics.

46 Parrish, D. (2006), p. 106.

47 Grof, S. (1983), p. 14.

48 Quoted in Carr, Jane. *The Lives and Theories of Two Great Creative Giants: Carl Jung and David Bohm.* (2003). Saybrook Research Institute and Graduate School, MA dissertation.

49 Corbett (2012), p. 42.

50 Corbett (2012), p. 43.

51 Jacobi, J. (1971), quoted in Carr (2003), p. 29.

52 Peat, F. David (1987), p. 167.

53 Jung, C. G. (1959), pp. 151–154; Noll, R. (1997). Noll makes an argument that Jung fabricated the evidence for his theory of a collective unconscious by relying principally on the so-called *Solar Phallus Man* story recounted from a patient he claimed was his, but who was, in fact, a patient of an associate, J. Honegger. Noll also discredits the biography *Memories, Dreams, Reflections* as a distorted attempt to sacralize Jung's personality which was written principally by Aniela Jaffé, one of his closest confidants.

54 Von Franz (1980), p. 36.

55 Corbett (2012), p. 44.

56 Carr, p. 31.

57 Corbett (2012).

58 Jung (1969), p. 101.

59 Corbett (2012), pp. 42–43.

60 Taylor, Jeremy (1992), p. 239.

61 Ponte, Diogo Valadas and Lothar Schäfer. (2013). Carl Gustav Jung, Quantum Physics and Spiritual Mind: A Mystical Vision of the Twenty-First Century. *Behavioral Sciences*, 3, pp. 601–618.

62 Davies, P. (1992), pp. 15–16.

63 Peat, F. David (1987), p. 168.

64 Singer, June (1984), pp. 1–12.

65 Bohm, David (1980), p. 237.

66 Kastrup, B. (2019). Kastrup argues that there is no actual boundary between the micro and macro worlds; the distinction between the two is purely arbitrary, and therefore the entanglement observed in quantum physics has validity in the macro world.

67 Goswami, A. (1995), p. 9.

68 Radin, D. (2006), p. 14.

69 Capra, F. (2010), p. 138; Corbett, L. (2019), p. 42. Corbett, a psychiatrist, applies the notion of connectedness at the level of the psyche where he states: "Though we usually have the sense of being separate individuals, we are all none-theless connected to each other at the transpersonal level of the psyche."

70 Peat (1987), p. 169.

71 Radin (2006), p. 254.

72 Bohm (1980), pp. 188–189.

73 Keutzer, C. S. (1983), pp. 353–367.

74 Carr, Jane (2003), p. 40.

75 Keutzer (1983), p. 356.

76 Parrish, D. (2006), pp. 70, 77.

77 Parrish, D. (2006), pp. 121–122.

78 See, for example, Laszlo, E. (2004); Sheldrake, R. (2006). Morphic fields. *World Futures*, *62*(1–2), 31–41. The problem of where memory is stored is par-ticularly troublesome in trying to explain how individuals who have near-death experiences can recall those experiences when their brain shows no activity.

79 Carr (2003), p. 30. Carr (2003) has noted similarities between Jung's ideas of the enfolding and reemerging of archetypes into the unconscious and Bohm's theories.

80 Maddox, J. (1981), pp. 245–246.

81 Grof (1983), p. 25.

82 Carr (2003), p. 47; Ramachandran, V. S., & Hirstein, W. (1998), pp. 1603–1630. This paper provides support for Sheldrake's morphogenetic fields in a serious study on the phantom limb phenomenon. The limbs continue to be felt after they have been amputated, suggesting that an explanation may be found through the hypothesis of morphogenetic fields.

83 Parrish (2006), p. 151.

84 Singer (1984), p. 7.

85 Sheldrake, R. (2003), p. 263.

86 Sheldrake, R. (2003), p. 265. Evidence for psychokinesis includes experimental proof of people influencing random number generators and evidence of the beneficial effects of prayer at a distance.

87 Heisenberg, W., & Bond, B. (1958), p. 140. *Physics and Philosophy: The Revolution in Modern Science.* Harper Collins Publishers, Inc.

88 Edgcombe, D. (2003), p. 15; Smith, H. (2000), p. 65. Smith conflates the terms "Ultimate Reality" and "God."

89 Physicist and Nobel Laureate Richard Feynman had this to say about quantum physics: "It is my task to convince you *not* to turn away because you don't understand it [quantum electrodynamics]. You see, my physics students don't understand it either. That is because *I* don't understand it. Nobody does."

90 Miller, A. (2010), p. 225; Irwin, L. (2015). Mystical Knowledge and Near-Death Experience. In *Death, Dying, and Mysticism* (pp. 153–175). Palgrave Macmillan, New York. Irwin argues that reports of mystical experiences are influenced by language, tradition, and social-cultural factors, and that there are, therefore "multiple mysticisms...and no universal core mysticism."

91 Sheldrake, R. (1987), pp. 9–25.

92 Kurtz, P. (1986), p. 92.

93 Kurtz, P. (1986), p. 94.

94 If an observer is required to convert a mere probability into a physical particle, doesn't that, in essence, lend support to the reality of psychokinesis (PK), which is the ability to influence a physical system without physical interaction? Narasimhan, A., Chopra, D., & Kafatos, M. C. (2019). "The Nature of the Heisenberg-Von Neumann Cut: Enhanced Orthodox Interpretation of Quantum Mechanics." *Activitas Nervosa Superior*, *61*(1–2), 12–17. This paper argues that "complete reality" consists of both space-time and not-space-time; the hidden reality may be thought of as the not-space-time component of reality. Such dialetheism is characteristic of Buddhist philosophy: see Deguchi, Y., Garfield, J. L., & Priest, G. (2008).

95 Rosenblum, B., & Kuttner, F. (2011), pp. 11, 103.

96 Carroll, Sean and Alan Wallace. (2017). A quote dubiously attributed to Lord Kelvin that "[t]here is nothing new to be discovered in physics now. All that remains is more and more precise measurement," sounds foolish now, but Carroll might be making the same mistake with his statement in reference to ESP: "We know that there aren't new particles or forces out there yet to be discovered that would support them. Not simply because we have not found them yet, but because we definitely would have found them if they had the right characteristics to give us the requisite powers." His statement is, at best, naïve. See the recent paper "*A Fifth Fundamental Force Could Really Exist, but We Haven't Found it Yet,*" https://phys.org/news/2019-11-fundamental-havent.html. Accessed March 17, 2020.

97 Bonchek, L. I. (2016).

98 Corbett (2012), p. 3.

99 Bohm, D. (2004), p. 3

100 Jung, C. G., & Jaffé, Aniela. (1963), p. 304.

101 Radin, D. (2006), p. 221.

102 Wilhelm, Richard, trans. (1967), p. xxiv.

103 Talbot, M. (1992), p. 40.

104 Russell, B. (1912). On the notion of cause. In *Proceedings of the Aristotelian society* (Vol. 13, pp. 1–26). Aristotelian Society, Wiley.

105 Bohm, D. (2004), p. 8.

106 Wilhelm, H. (Ed.). (2011), p. xxiii.

107 Wilhelm, H. (Ed.). (2011).

108 Miller, A. I. (2010), p. 190.

109 Jung, C.G. 1960.

110 Capra, Fritjof, p. 137.

111 Capra, Fritjof, p. 138.

112 Von Franz, M. L. (2001).

113 McFadden, J. (2002), pp. 172–173.

114 Mansfield, Victor, p. 122.

115 Jung, C. G. (2014).

116 Beitman, B. D. (2011).

117 Beitman, B. D. (2011).

118 Diaconis, Persi and Frederick Mosteller, "Methods for Studying Coincidences," *Journal of the American Statistical Association*, Vol. 84, No. 408, pp. 853–63.

119 Koestler, Arthur (1972), p. 107.

120 Beitman, B. D. (2011), p. 567.

121 See, for example: http://www.plosone.org/article/info:doi/10.1371/journal.pone.0006405 and http://www.nature.com/nature/journal/v467/n7318/full/nature09491.html. There is an intuitive attractiveness to the theories of Lamarck; I address this more fully in the chapter on evolution.

122 Combs, A., & Holland, M. (1990), p. 3.

123 Nechita, Elena. (2010), pp. 49–54.

124 Townley, John and Robert Schmidt. Paul Kammerer and the Law of Seriality. http://www.astrococktail.com/PDF/PAULKA_x007E_1.pdf. Accessed 6/15/2019.

125 https://www.psychologytoday.com/us/blog/connecting-coincidence/201703/seriality-vs-synchronicity-kammerer-vs-jung. Accessed 6/15/2019.

126 Beitman, B. D. (2011), p. 567.

127 http://www.translorial.com/essays/untranslatable-words-serendipity/

128 Laval, R. (2013). *Making sense of synchronicity* (Doctoral dissertation, University of Northern British Columbia), p. 3.

129 https://en.wikipedia.org/wiki/Serendipity.

130 https://wikidiff.com/serendipity/synchronicity.

131 Beitman, B. D. (2011), pp. 567.

132 Colman, A. M. (2015). *A Dictionary of Psychology*. Oxford Quick Reference. Von Franz, M. L. (1998), p. 32. Von Franz states, "If you observe your dreams regularly, you will see that such meaningful coincidences of outer and inner events do occur with relative frequency." These are instances of synchronicity.

133 Jung, C. G. 1960, para. 824–825.

134 Mansfield, p. 46. See Storm, L. (1999). For a more detailed discussion and an exploration of the term "meaning" when discussing synchronicity.

135 Vallee, J., & Strieber, W. (1988), p. 255. French physicist Costa de Beauregard stated: "It must be in the nature of probability to serve as the operational link between objective and subjective, between matter and psychism." This seems to imply a relationship between probability and synchronicity, as they both mediate between the objective and subjective.

136 Combs and Holland (1996), p. 11.

137 Jung, C. G. (1960), p. 506. See also Radin (1997), p. 173 in which synchronicity's relationship to field consciousness is discussed.

138 von Franz (1980), pp. 78–79.

139 Atmanspacher, H. (2014), pp. 181–188.

140 Russell, B. (2000).

141 Jung, C. G. (1960), p. 485.

142 Atmanspacher, H. (2014), pp. 181–188.

143 Bohm, D. (1990). A new theory of the relationship of mind and matter. *Philosophical Psychology*, *3*(2–3), 271–286.

144 Atmanspacher, H. (2014), p. 184.

145 There are numerous references to Pauli's contribution to Jung's work on the psyche in Jung, C. G. (1960). For example, see Peat (1987) and Mansfield (1995), to name just two. Treatments by psychotherapists include those by Progroff (1973) and Hopcke (1997).

146 Peat, F. D. (1987), p. 24.

147 Miller, A. (2010), p. xviii.

148 Von Franz, M. L. (2001).

149 Von Franz, M. L. (2001), p. 271.

150 Dictionary, S. O. E. (2007). Shorter Oxford English Dictionary.

151 Beitman, B. D. (2011), p. 569.

152 Cameron, M. A. (2004), p. 105.

153 Corbett, (2012), p. 104. Corbett notes that Jesus said that the Kingdom of God (spiritual reality) "is present everywhere, even if we do not see it…We may experience it as…synchronicity, or other types of encounters, but it is always present."

154 Peat, F. D. (1987), p. 22.

155 Bird, W. R. (1989), Vol. I, p. 15.

156 Bird, W. R. (1989), Vol. I, p. 18.

157 Bird, W. R. (1989), Vol. I, p. 17.

158 Sheldrake, R. (2011), p. 19.

159 The "big bang" theory conveniently ignores that quantum theory dictates that in order for energy in the form of waves to collapse into matter, there must be an observer—perhaps an intelligent designer!

160 Bird, W. R. (1989), Vol. I, p. 436.

161 Cooper, P. D. (2017), p. 62.

162 Dawkins, R. (1996), p. 29. Interestingly, Dawkins is widely recognized as a leading proponent of neo-Darwinian evolutionary theory.

163 Meyer, Stephen C. (2013), p. 171; Taylor, G. R. (1983), p. 4. Murray Eden showed that "if it required a mere six mutations to bring about adaptive change, this would occur by chance only once in a billion years—while, if two dozen genes were involved, it would require 10,000,000,000 years, which is much longer than the age of the earth."

164 Eden, M. (1967), quoted in Bird, W. R. (1989), Vol. II, p. 87.

165 Bird, W. R. (1989), Vol. I, p. 51.

166 Bird, W. R. (1989), Vol. I, p. 51.

167 Darwin, Charles (1872), p. 290.

168 Meyer (2013), p. 23.

169 Meyer, Stephen C. (2013), p. 3.

170 Losch, A. (Ed.). (2017), p. 79.

171 Bohm, David (1980), p. 269–270. Bohm suggests that successive living forms unfold creatively. "Later members are not completely derivable from what came earlier…this unfoldment cannot be properly understood without considering the immense multidimensional reality of which it is a projection." This multidimensional reality is the ultimate reality that exists beyond our perception.

172 Tirard, S. (2017). J. B. S. Haldane and the origin of life. *Journal of Genetics*, *96*(5), 735–739. Haldane, J. B. S. (2002), p. 286. Two years before he "supposed how life originated," Haldane was less confident about the nature of our world. He stated: "Now, my own suspicion is that the universe is not only queerer than we suppose, but queerer than we *can* suppose"!

173 https://www.sciencedaily.com/releases/2010/02/100202101245.htm, accessed December 18, 2019.

174 Boyden, A. (1942). Systematic serology: a critical appreciation. *Physiological Zoology*, *15*(2), 109–145. Quoted in Bird, W. R. (1989). *Origin of Species Revisited: Science* (Vol. 1). Philosophical Library, p. 143.

175 Meyer (2013), p. 51.

176 Meyer (2013), p. 52.

177 The scientific method consists of "systematic observation, measurement, and experiment, and the formulation, testing, and modification of hypotheses."

https://www.lexico.com/en/definition/scientific_method. Accessed Nov. 12, 2019.

178 Axe, D. (2016). It is not only my intuition about life having been designed, but also that of many other scientists and philosophers who have dared to venture out of the materialistic paradigm which continues to lose influence.

179 Fodor, J., & Piattelli-Palmarini, M. (2011), pp. 1, 96–100. The authors find considerable difficulty with "adaptationism," which Darwin thought would be a refined theory of evolution.

180 Sheldrake, R. (1995), p. 137.

181 Laszlo, E. (1987), p. 14.

182 Meyer (2013), p. 14.

183 Smith, H. (2000), p. 66.

184 Wikipedia. https://en.wikipedia.org/wiki/Forbidden_Archeology, Accessed February 4, 2020.

185 Cremo, M. A. (2003), pp. 9–10.

186 Bird, W. R. (1989), Vol. II, p. 112.

187 Meyer (2013), pp. 185–186.

188 Dawkins, Richard. (1986), p. 45.

189 Dawkins, Richard. (1996), p. 5.

190 https://www.lexico.com/en/definition/teleological_argument, November 21, 2019.

191 Lennox, J. G. (1993), pp. 409–421.

192 Lennox, J. G. (1993).

193 Mayr, E. (1988). *Toward a new philosophy of biology: Observations of an evolutionist* (No. 211). Harvard University Press, p. 43.

194 Mayr, E. (1988), p. 43.

195 Mayr, E. (1988), p. 241.

196 Bird, W. R. (1989), Vol. II, p. 308.

197 Burkhardt, R., & Richard, W. (2011), p. 33.

198 Szyf, M. (2014), p. 2.

199 Sheldrake, R. (1995), pp. 133–134.

200 Meyer (2013), p. 330.

201 Foster, J. B. (1964). Evolution of mammals on islands. *Nature, 202*(4929), 234.

202 Koonin, E. V., & Wolf, Y. I. (2009). Is evolution Darwinian or/and Lamarckian? *Biology direct, 4*(1), 42.

203 Kutschera, U. (2003). A comparative analysis of the Darwin-Wallace papers and the development of the concept of natural selection. *Theory in Biosciences, 122*(4), 343–359. Bergson, H. (2010). *Creative evolution*. Indo-European Publishing. Here Bergson makes an important point about the resistance to anything even slightly referred to as Lamarckism: "After having been affirmed as a dogma, the transmissibility of acquired character has been no less dogmatically denied," p. 46.

204 Taylor, G. R. (1983), p. 20. Taylor also states: "In studying evolution, many scientists—paleontologists especially—have felt forced to accept the existence of some directive force and have felt it impossible to assign the many seemingly purposeful developments to chance," and "While some scientists have felt forced to postulate some directive influence in evolution, others froth at the mouth at the mere idea. This is because they fear that we shall revert to believing in a divine plan," pp. 5–6.

205 Sheldrake, R. (1995), p. 56.

206 Sheldrake, A. R. (1980). Three approaches to biology. 1. The mechanistic theory of life. *Theoria to Theory*, *14*, 125–144.

207 Sheldrake, R. (2011), p. xvi.

208 Hoffman, D. (2019), p. 76.

209 Hoffman, D. (2019), pp. xii–xiii. Hoffman further argues: "We see none of reality as it is," p. 20. Blackmore, Susan J. (1984). Blackmore has a theory similar to that of Hoffman, although she argues that the mind creates a model of reality, and when sensory input changes, the mind creates another model from memory and imagination. She believes that this theory explains what is happening in OBEs; Hoffman seems to believe that evolution has created his "icons" of objective reality.

210 Smith, H. (2000), p. 74. Perhaps he will miss the lion, but Smith argues that the fully realized human being is one for whom the doors of perception have been cleansed.

211 Bird, W. R. (1989), Vol. II, p. 89.

212 Arthur, K. (1967), p. 127.

213 Dossey, L., Greyson, B., Sturrock, P. A., & Tucker, J. B. (2011), pp. 4697–4711.

214 Biologist R.

215 Fechner, G. T., & Lowrie, W. (1947), p. 186.

216 Planck, Max. (1959).

217 Searle, J. R. (1992), pp. 3–4.

218 Dossey, L., Greyson, B., Sturrock, P. A., & Tucker, J. B. (2011). Consciousness—What Is It? *Journal of Cosmology*, *14*, pp. 4697–4711.

219 Dossey, L., Greyson, B., Sturrock, P. A., & Tucker, pp. 4697–4711.

220 Goswami, A. (1995), p. 17. Epiphenomenalism seems to confuse cause and effect with correlations.

221 McFadden (2002), p. 158.

222 Kumar, M. (2008), p. 321.

223 Theise, N. D., & Kafatos, M. (2013). Sentience everywhere: complexity theory, panpsychism & the role of sentience in self-organization of the universe. *Journal of Consciousness Exploration & Research*, *4*(4).

224 Wolf, A. F. (1994), p. 90.

225 Lewin, Roger (1980); Libet, B. (2004). Lewin's paper discusses Lorber's findings that an individual can apparently function quite normally with a massive amount of brain loss. Libet's experiments showed a delay between a stimulus to the brain and the conscious awareness of that stimulus, which he suggested was evidence of a conscious mental field.

226 Skrbina, D. (2017).

227 Bayne, T., Cleeremans, A., & Wilken, P. (Eds.). (2014), p. 254.

228 Honderich, T. (Ed.). (2005).

229 Stanford Encyclopedia of Philosophy. https://plato.stanford.edu/entries/panpsychism/#DefiPanp, accessed December 21, 2019.

230 Koch, C. (2014). Ubiquitous minds. *Scientific American Mind*, *25*(1), 26–29.

231 Kafatos, M., Tanzi, R. E., & Chopra, D. (2011). How consciousness becomes the physical universe. *Journal of Cosmology*, *14*, 1–11. The authors acknowledge that the title of their paper is "provocative."

232 Smith, H. (2000), p. 70.

233 Dreyfus, Georges, (2010).

234 Godfrey-Smith, P. (2016), p. 79.

235 Theise, N. D., & Kafatos, M. (2013).

236 Theise, N. D., & Kafatos, M. (2013), p. 379.

237 Theise, N. D., & Kafatos, M. (2013), p. 385.

238 Huxley, A. (1990), p. 22; Morse, M. (1999). The right temporal lobe and associated limbic lobe structures act as the biological interface with an interconnected universe. Morse, a medical doctor, has stated "I speculate that our right temporal lobe allows humans to interact with a timeless space-less 'non-local' reality...The existence of such a reality is predicted by modern quantum theoretical physics."

239 Huxley, A. (1990), p. 59.

240 What Plants Talk About: https://www.youtube.com/watch?v=yfDli9zA2v8. Accessed November 21, 2019. At 28.04–28.13: "one could interpret that as evidence of self-awareness [because] if they're not able to perceive themselves everything goes wrong."

241 Facco, E., Agrillo, C., & Greyson, B. (2015). Epistemological implications of near-death experiences and other nonordinary mental expressions: Moving beyond the concept of altered state of consciousness. *Medical Hypotheses*, *85*(1), p. 87.

242 Lewin, Roger. "Is Your Brain Really Necessary?" *Science, New Series*, Vol. 2010, No. 4475, pp. 1232–1234.

243 Feuillet, Lionel. "Brain of a White-Collar Worker." *The Lancet*, Vol. 30, 2007.

244 Theise, N. D., & Kafatos, M. (2013), p. 387.

245 Gribbin, J. (1984), p. 164.

246 Gribbin, J. (1984), p. 171.

247 Kafatos, M., Tanzi, R. E., & Chopra, D. (2011). How consciousness becomes the physical universe. *Journal of Cosmology*, *14*, 1–11.

248 Wikipedia. https://en.wikipedia.org/wiki/Herbert_Spencer_Jennings. Accessed January 13, 2020.

249 Jennings, H. S. (1906).

250 What Plants Talk About: https://www.youtube.com/watch?v=yfDli9zA2v8. Accessed November 21, 2019. This is a fascinating, scientific analysis of the behavior of plants in their environment. Anyone watching this presentation will come away with a profound appreciation of the life of plants, and perhaps even become more receptive to the idea that plants exhibit something akin to what we call "consciousness."'

251 Koch, C. (2014), pp. 26–29. Koch exhibits a willingness to consider the Buddhist doctrines with an open mind. The Dalai Lama has stated that "[i]f science proves that some belief of Buddhism is wrong, then Buddhism will have to change." Rupert Sheldrake has often raised the question as to whether the sun and the entire universe are conscious. See, for example, "Is the Sun Conscious" at *Sheldrake.org*.

252 https://en.wikipedia.org/wiki/Integrated_information_theory. Accessed August 4, 2020.

253 Safina, Carl (2016). What Animals are Thinking and Feeling and Why It Should Matter. https://www.youtube.com/results?search_query=what+animals+are+thinking+and+feeling+and+why+it+should+matter. This excellent YouTube video discussion focuses on the consciousness of animals and why it matters. See also Trewavas, A. J., & Baluška, F. (2011).

254 Sneddon, L. U. (2006). Ethics and welfare: pain perception in fish. *Bulletin of the European Association of Fish Pathologists*, *26*(1), 6–10; Braithwaite, V. (2010). *Do Fish Feel Pain?* Oxford University Press. Note that there is no unanimity on the question of pain in fish.

255 Wikipedia. https://en.wikipedia.org/wiki/Speciesism. Accessed January 14, 2020; Miralles, A., Raymond, M., & Lecointre, G. (2019). The authors note that the greater the genetic distance or evolutionary time separating us from a given organism, the weaker our predisposition to connect emotionally with that organism. It's possible speciesism has a biological basis.

256 Homer, p. 531.

257 Cockburn, D. (1994). Human beings and giant squids. *Philosophy*, *69*(268), 135–150. I would add that often in prayers given to a congregation, there is an exhortation "that those in public service use their position and influence to promote laws that honor the dignity of all human life." I strongly believe that it is the dignity of *all living things* that should be honored.

258 Long, A. (1995), pp. 119–121.

259 Long, A. (1995), p. 119.

260 Hume dismissed the idea of a "self." If that is so, it seems duplicitous to use it as a basis to deny the consciousness of nonhuman animals.

261 Long, A. (1995), p. 121.

262 De Waal, F. B. (2012), p. 874.

263 Trewavas, A. J., & Baluška, F. (2011), p. 1223. The authors found characteristics of primitive organisms that showed sophisticated behaviors which give evidence for some kind of self-awareness and intelligence.

264 Huxley, A. (2009), p. 161.

265 Trigg, D. (2004). Schopenhauer and the sublime pleasure of tragedy. *Philosophy and Literature*, *28*(1), 165–179.

266 Darwin, C. (1892). *The Formation of Vegetable Mould through the Action of Worms: With Observations on their Habits* (Vol. 37). Appleton.

267 Draper, Electa. (2009). https://www.denverpost.com/2009/05/15/canine-emotions-raise-theological-questions/.

268 Evans-Wentz, W. Y. (1958), p. 11; https://www.usatoday.com/story/news/nation-now/2014/12/12/pope-francis-dogs-can-go-to-heaven/20296955/. Accessed July 7, 2020.

269 Sheldrake, R. (2011), p. 5.

270 Sheldrake, R. (2011), p. 24.

271 Sheldrake, R. (2011), p. 114.

272 Sheldrake, R. (2011), p. 110.

273 Moncrieff, M. M. (1951), pp. 47–48. Ring, K., & Cooper, S. (2008), p. 108. In investigating apparent visual awareness in blind individuals who experience OBEs and NDEs, Ring and Cooper consider such phenomena "transcendental awareness." I include this reference because of its proximate parallel with Moncrieff's clairvoyant theory of perception.

274 Moncrieff, M. M. (1951), pp. 51–54; Marais, E. (2009); Hoffman, D. (2019), p. 187. Hoffman apparently hasn't read Moncrieff, so concludes it would be difficult to probe the consciousness of an ant.

275 Mancuso, Stefano. (2018), pp. 12–13.

276 Mancuso, Stefano. (2015). https://www.youtube.com/watch?v=gBGt5OeAQFk. Accessed February 19, 2020.

277 Gagliano, M., Renton, M., Depczynski, M., & Mancuso, S. (2014). Experience teaches plants to learn faster and forget slower in environments where it matters. *Oecologia*, *175*(1), 63–72.

278 Lindsay, W. L. (1876). Mind in plants. *Journal of Mental Science*, *21*(96), 513–532.

279 Lindsay, W. L. (1876), p. 520.

280 James, W. (1902), p.705. Fechner, G. T. (2005). William James, in the introduction to this book, notes that Fechner believed "inner experience is the reality, and that matter is but a form in which inner experiences may appear to one another when they affect each other from the outside." Fechner also held the view that "inner experience…and the physical universe are co-eternal aspects of one self-same reality, much the same as concave and convex are aspects of one curve."

281 Webster, Bayard (1983). The Plant Biologists Turn Over a New Leaf. *New York Times*, June 12.

282 Tompkins, P., & Bird, C. (1973).

283 Dillon, J. (Ed.). (1991), p. 31. Plotinus (204/5-270 C.E.) is considered the founder of Neoplatonism. In his fourth tractate, he states: "Those that deny the happy life to the plants on the ground that they lack sensation are really denying it to all living things."

284 Tompkins, P. (1997), back cover.

285 Milton, R. (1996), p. 109.

286 Nagel, A. H. (1997). Are plants conscious? *Journal of Consciousness Studies*, *4*(3), 215–230; Michael Pollan (2013). The intelligent plant. *New Yorker*, 93.

287 Sheldrake, R. (1987). Part I: Mind, memory, and archetype morphic resonance and the collective unconscious. *Psychological Perspectives*, *18*(1), 9–25; Penfield, W. (1975).

288 It is not certain the degree to which cells in the brain have a cyclical life. Some cells may last as long as the body.

289 Pearsall, P., Schwartz, G. E., & Russek, L. G. (2000). Changes in heart transplant recipients that parallel the personalities of their donors. *Integrative Medicine*, *2*(2–3), 65–72.

290 Zukov, G. (1979), p. 200.

291 Sheldrake, R. (2011), pp. 250–252.

292 Edrington, D., p. 7.

293 Hoffman, D. (2019), p. 6.

294 Hoffman, D. (2019), p. 9.

295 Hoffman, D. (2019), p. 7.

296 Pinto, Y., et al. (2017), p. 1235.

297 Colman, Andrew M. (2006); Corbett (2012), p. 120. Corbett, referring to Christou's *Logos of the Soul*, notes that "what we call body, mind, and soul are different orders of reality, each with its own perspective." These "perspectives" constitute the whole person.

298 Strasburger, H., & Waldvogel, B. (2015). Sight and blindness in the same person: Gating in the visual system. *PsyCh Journal*, *4*(4), 178–185. Discussed in Kastrup, B. (2018). The universe in consciousness. *Journal of Consciousness Studies*, *25*(5–6), 125–155.

299 Goleman, D. (1988). Probing the enigma of multiple personality. *New York Times*, *25*, C1.

300 Kastrup, B. (2014), p. 192.

301 Evans-Wentz, W. Y. (1968), p. xxx. Evans-Wentz preceded Kastrup with the same thought: "In other words it is just as possible that our mind is nothing but a perceptible manifestation of a Universal Mind."

302 Kastrup, B. (2014), p. 195.

303 Ludwig, A. M. (1966), pp. 225–234.

304 Garcia-Romeu, Albert P. and Tart, Charles T. (2013), p. 123.

305 James, W. (1987), p. 349.

306 Not to be forgotten are the rituals of shamans. Like the effect of entheogens, the reciting of mantras, and the dance of dervishes, they serve to loosen the grip of the ego on the mind and allow the mind to experience the Ultimate Reality or God.

307 Webb, Mark (2017), p. 2. Webb notes that Saint Paul, Moses, Muhammad, and others had religious experiences which were "unsought, not as the result of some deliberate practice undertaken to produce an experience." They exemplify what I mean by "gratuitous experiences of the sacred.'"

308 Otto, R. (1958), pp. 17, 32, 37. Jaffé, A. (1979), p. 69. Jaffé notes that the illumination in gratuitous experiences of the sacred are not to be found in either "consciousness nor in the intellect; it corresponds to an 'inner light' or proceeds from it. Enlightenment cannot be achieved by will or force: it comes upon man as a grace or inspiration from an autonomous, unknown source." Jaffé was a protégé of Jung.

309 Emerson, R. W. (1983), p. 10. Pollan, M. (2019), p. 268 described his experience under the influence of psilocybin: "Instead of Emerson's transparent eyeball, egoless and one with all it beheld, I became a transparent ear, indistinguishable from the stream of sound that flooded my consciousness."

310 Garcia-Romeu, Albert P. and Charles T. Tart (2013), p. 121.

311 Huxley, A. (1990), p. 23.

312 Corbett, (2012), p. 12.

313 Jung, C. G., & Jaffé, Aniela. (1963), pp. 289–293. Jung's experience could also be considered a near-death experience.

314 James, W. (1987), pp. 347–348; Wulf, D. M. (2014), p. 372.

315 James, W. (1987), pp. 66, 70.

316 James, W. (1987), p. 36.

317 Smith, H. (1991), p. 387.

318 Teasdale, W. (2001), p. 17.

319 Teasdale, W. (2001), pp. 212–216.

320 Webb, Mark (2017), p. 1

321 Teasdale, W. (2001), p. 212.

322 Huxley, A. (2009). *Beliefs*. In *The Perennial Philosophy*, p. 15.

323 Phipps, Carter. (2000). Also consider Pollan's statement after ingesting hallucinogenics: "This sense of merging into some larger totality is of course one of the hallmarks of the mystical experience; our sense of individuality and separateness hinges on a bounded self and a clear demarcation between subject and object. But all that may be a mental construction, a kind of illusion—just as the Buddhists have been trying to tell us." Pollan, (2019), p. 305.

324 Perez-De-Albeniz, A., & Holmes, J., pp. 49–58.

325 Radin, D. (2006), p. 277.

326 Braud, W. G. (1990).

327 Krippner, S., & Faith, L. (2001), pp. 73–82.

328 LaBerge, Stephen (1985), p. 228.

329 Prof. Ralph Metzner has described objective as subjective plus one more.

330 LaBerge, Stephen (1985), p. 228.

331 LaBerge (1985), p. 228. LaBerge also states "According to Buddhist doctrine, the entire universe of forms, or separate existence, is an illusory appearance or 'dream'...all experiences are necessarily mental representations and, as the subjective products of our brains, are thus of the same nature as dreams," p. 262. The illusion of separate existence agrees with quantum theory.

332 Vaitl, D., et. al., p. 101.

333 Voss, U., Holzmann, R., Tuin, I., & Hobson, A. J. (2009), pp. 1191–1200; Vaitl, D., et al. p. 102; Von Franz, M. L. (1998), p. xv. Von Franz erroneously claims, "As is generally known, we cannot manipulate dreams." Clearly, lucid dreams allow the dreamer complete control of content.

334 LaBerge, Stephen. (1985), pp. 21–23.

335 Talbot, Michael. (1991), p. 3. For the sake of economy, I prefer to think of there being only one Ultimate Reality with many attributes.

336 Taylor, Jeremy, (1992), p. 27. Taylor believes all creativity arises from deep in the unconscious and dreams enable that creativity to enter the consciousness upon awakening.

337 LaBerge, (1985), p. 26.

338 Corbett, L. (2019), p. 26.

339 Shlain, L. (1993), p. 224. Shlain discusses how Picasso the artist and Einstein the physicist were both exploring the new ideas about space and time. Aided by Freud's *The Interpretation of Dreams*, artists began to seek creative ideas in their subconscious. The new movement built upon these ideas was named "*sur*realism, which means *above* reality." Bulkeley, K. (Ed.). (2016), p. 167. "Responding to a question about where he gets his ideas for songs, [Billy] Joel replied that all his songs come from dreams."

340 Faraday, A. (1976), p. 160.

341 Lewis, M., & Spignesi, S. J. (2009), p. 23.

342 Jung (1969), p. 306.

343 Corbett (2012), p. 43.

344 Taylor, Jeremy (1992), p. 46.

345 Taylor, Jeremy (1992), p. 48.

346 Bulkeley, K., & Bulkeley, P. (2006), p. 72.

347 Smith, H. (2000), p. 78.

348 Smith, H. (2000), p. 80.

349 Smith, H. (2000), pp. xvi–xvii. Dr. Rick Strassman prefers the term "psychedelic" to "entheogen" when a substance is used recreationally rather than in a ritualistic setting: https://theconsciousresistance.com/dr-rick-strassman-on-the-reality-and-fantasy-of-dmt/. Accessed August 4, 2020.

350 Evans-Wentz, W. Y. (1958), p. 19: "Reality in its true essence, as Undifferentiated Absoluteness, which is called the Voidness."

351 Smith, H. (2000), p. 12.

352 Smith, H. (2000), p. 65.

353 Pollan (2019), p. 353.

354 Pollan (2019), p. 173.

355 Pollan, M. (2019), p. 161.

356 Pollan (2019), p. 288.

357 Blanke, O., & Mohr, C. (2005), p. 186.

358 Green, C. E., & McCreery, C. (1975) p. 112.

359 Socrates, Pliny, and Plotinus all gave descriptions of out-of-body experiences. Plotinus wrote: "Many times it has happened: lifted out of the body into myself; becoming external to all other things and self-centered; beholding a marvelous beauty; then, more-than ever, assured of community with the loftiest order... acquiring identity with the divine." Eighth Tractate in Dillon, J. (Ed.). (1991), p. 334.

360 Jung, C. G. (1960), p. 507. Jung describes a case in which a woman describes her out-of-body experience while in a coma. This report was in Jung's essay on synchronicity, which was written twenty years before Moody's landmark work.

361 Holden, J. M. (2017), p. 80.

362 Siegel, R. K. (1980). The psychology of life after death. *American Psychologist, 35*(10), 921; Schwenn, H. (2014), p. 65. Schwenn found approximately 16.5 percent of experiencers reported being attached to a silver cord or beam of light.

363 Knox, C. (1979). *The Body Mind Relationship and Parapsychology* (Doctoral dissertation, University of Surrey, United Kingdom), p. 145.

364 Rinpoche, S. (1990), pp. 192–203.

365 Rinpoche, S. (1990), p. 201.

366 Woodhouse, M. B. (1994), p. 13. Perhaps this is that force: *A Fifth Fundamental Force Could Really Exist, but We Haven't Found It Yet*, https://phys.org/news/2019-11-fundamental-havent.html. Accessed March 17, 2020.

367 Besant, A. (1896), p. 84; Jonas, H. (1986), p. 122. Jonas recounts Spinoza's doctrine of one substance with different attributes. This may explain the relationship between the material body and the subtle body.

368 Arnette, J. K. (1997). *An interactionist theory of mind and body* (Doctoral dissertation, Colorado State University), p. 3.

369 Wikipedia. https://www.google.com/search?q=dualism&oq=dualism&aqs=chrome..69i57j0l6.1375j0j4&sourceid=chrome&ie=UTF-8. Accessed July 7, 2020.

370 "Descartes never says that anything is non-physical, and this is not because he does not use the word physics; for Descartes, God is physics" (Edwards).

371 Jonas, H. (1986).

372 Arnette, J. K. (1997), p. 8.

373 Schwerin, A. (2007), p. 1; Montero, B. (1999); The body problem. *Nous, 33*(2), 183–200.

374 For an excellent discussion of the comparison and contrast between Hume's "bundles" and the Buddhist doctrine of anatta, see Huxley, A. (2009), *The Perennial Philosophy*. HarperPerennial, p. 38.

375 von Franz, M. L. (2001), pp. 219–220.

376 von Franz 1980. pp. 78–79.

377 Stapp, H. P. (2011), p. 81.

378 Stapp, H. P. (2011), p. 81.

379 Stapp, H. P. (2011), p. 2; Stapp, H. P. (1996), pp. 194–210.

380 Sheldrake, R. (2012), p. 126.

381 Cooper, J. M., & Hutchinson, D. S. (Eds.) (1997), Vol I, Phaedo 65c.

382 Wilson, C. (2011). *Afterlife: An Investigation*. Doubleday, p. 63.

383 Von Franz, M. L. (1998). *On Dreams and Death*. Open Court, p.144.

384 Von Franz, M. L. (1999); Capra, F. (2010).

385 Steiner, R. (2014), p. 142. Steiner claims "There are really seven different types of etheric body in human beings."

386 Blackmore, S. J. (1982), pp. 16–17.

387 Blackmore, S. J. (1982), pp. 14–15.

388 Blackmore, S. J. (1982), p. 10.

389 Edgcombe, D. (2003), p. 21.

390 Edgcombe, D. (2003), p. 28 quoting Schmicker. M. (2000), p. 157. Edgcombe is discussing NDEs, but her comments apply equally to OBEs. Cardeña, E. E and Alvarado, Carlos S. (2014), pp. 179–180. The authors, citing Tart, note that while an OBE can be experienced in an NDE, the experiences are not identical.

391 LaBerge, (1985), p. 229.

392 Faraday, A. (1976), p. 341.

393 Edgcombe, D. (2003), pp. 7–8.

394 Blackmore, S. J. (1988).

395 Cooper, J. M., & Hutchinson, D. S. (Eds.). (1997), Vol III, Republic 614b+.

396 Moody, R. A. (1975), p. 117.

397 Holden (2017), p. 80.

398 Chalmers, David (2014). https://www.youtube.com/watch?v=uhRhtFFhNzQ. Accessed December 28, 2019.

399 Irwin, L. (2015), p. 18.

400 Ring, K., & Cooper, S. (2008), p. 86.

401 Foster, R. D. (2010).

402 Moody, R. A. (1975).

403 Moody, R. A. (1975).

404 Betty, S. (2017). See the discussion in Chapter 5 concerning Dr. Lorber's discoveries about the functioning of individuals with a very small amount of brain matter.

405 Sabom, M. B. (1998), pp. 37–82; Smith, H. (2000), p. 13. In Smith's experience with mescaline, he described "Lights such as never were on land or sea."

406 Woerlee, G. M. (2011), pp. 3–25.

407 Greyson, B. (2010), p. 41.

408 Moody, R. A. (1975), pp. 84–85.

409 Palmieri, A., Calvo, V., Kleinbub, J. R., Meconi, F., Marangoni, M., Barilaro, P., & Sessa, P., p. 429.

410 Potts, M. (2012). Does N, N-Dimethyltryptamine (DMT) Adequately Explain Near-Death Experiences? *Journal of Near-Death Studies*, *31*(1), 3–23.

411 Evans-Wentz, W. Y. (1960), p. 35.

412 Sabom, M. B. (1982), p. 24.

413 Sabom, M. B. (1982), pp. 63–80.

414 Sabom, M. B. (1982), pp. 118–19.

415 Tietze, T. R. (1974), p. 340.

416 Wilson, C. (1988), p. 103.

417 Facco, E., Agrillo, C., & Greyson, B. (2015), p. 87.

418 Woodhouse, M. B. (1994), p. 2.

419 Vardamis, A. A., & Owens, J. E., pp. 203-217.

420 Green, C. (1968). *Out-of-the-Body Experiences* (Vol. 2). Institute of Psychophysical Research, p. 32–33. Schopenhauer, A. (1966), p. 22. Schopenhauer quotes Euler on perceptions: "I therefore believe that the sensations (of the senses) still contain something more than the philosophers imagine…They give to the soul not merely *ideas* of things, *but actually place before it* objects that exist outside it, although how this really happens we cannot conceive." This is supportive of the notion that the senses convey something more than the idea of things—they allow the mind to construct the objects themselves. This might help understand the perceptions of those experiencing not only NDEs, but OBEs and other altered states of consciousness.

421 Van Lommel, P. (2011), pp. 22–23; Holden, J. M., B. Greyson, & B. James, (2009), pp. 185–211.

422 Morse, M., & Perry, P.

423 Morse, p. 132.

424 Zaleski, C. (1988), pp. 124, 126.

425 Zajonc, A. (1995), p. 2.

426 Pollan, M. (2019), p. 71.

427 Huxley, A. (1990), p. 89.

428 Lynn, S. J., Fassler, O., & Knox, J. (2005).

429 Wilson, C. (1988), p. 58.

430 Hudson, T. J. (1902), p. 34.

431 Wilson, C. (1988), p. 57.

432 Hudson, T. J. (1902)., pp. 34–38.

433 Wilson, C. (1988), p. 58.

434 Jung, C. G., & Jaffé, Aniela (1963), p. 301.

435 Wilson, C. (1987), p. 114.

436 Leuba, J. H. (1915), p. 409–410.

437 Wilson, C. (1987), p. 158.

438 Wilson, C. (1987), p. 181.

439 Moody, R. A. (1992b), p. 112.

440 Bulkeley, K., & Bulkeley, P. (2006), p. 72. Bulkeley, relying on neuroscientists' claims, feels that "light is the origin of a fundamental sense of self."

441 Baroetto, G., p. 4; Strassman, R. (2000), p. 222. One of Strassman's subjects under the effects of DMT noted: "DMT sessions gave me the gift of truly

subjectively knowing the phenomenon described in [the Bardo]. Even greater is the gift of knowing that I have had practice dying and returning."

442 Evans-Wentz, W. Y. (1960), pp. 166–167 (footnote). "Meaning that the 'astral' or desire-body is incapable of ordinary injury."

443 Ho, D. Y. (1995), p. 121.

444 Easwaran, E. (2007), p. 78. The Hindu Katha Upanishad states "[t]he all-knowing Self was never born, nor will it die. Beyond cause and effect, this Self is eternal and immutable. When the body dies, the Self does not die." It is this view of the Self which is a major difference between Hinduism and Buddhism.

445 Ho, D. Y. (1995), p. 121.

446 Whitton, J. L., & Fisher, J. (1986), p. 3. This is a view shared with Schopenhauer.

447 Wilson, C. (1987), pp. 190–191.

448 Newton, M. (2010); Loftus, E. F. (1997).

449 Pyun, Y. D. (2015).

450 MacDonald et al. (1989), pp. 39, 61. Woolley, B. (2002), p. 155. In the biography of Dr. John Dee, the author notes that in a corner of his house was a mirror referred to as a "great perspective glass." Anyone who lunged at it saw "an effect so unsettling that many had claimed it must have magical powers." In Lewis Carroll's 1871 novel *Through the Looking Glass*, Alice enters another reality by climbing through a mirror.

451 Moody, R. A., and Paul Perry (1995), p. 44.

452 Moody, R. A. (1992), p. 84.

453 The psychomanteum offers a direct experience of a phenomenon which is secondhand at best when reported by a medium.

454 Moody, R. A. (1992), p. 85.

455 Moody, R. A., and Paul Perry (1995), p. 74; Roob, Alexander. (2006), p. 401. In a painting from the alchemical manuscript *Splendor Soils* a figure is shown holding a mirror, which is a reference to looking inside yourself. The androgynous figure holding the mirror represents the unity of opposites, which was a primary objective of the so-called *Great Work* of alchemy. Jung, C. G. (1953), p. 250. Jung's exploration of alchemy has relevance to Moody's psychomanteum in that during the practical work, the alchemist would experience visions (presumably by looking into the reflective liquid being prepared), which Jung considered projections of unconscious contents. See also p. 243 in this work for discussion of Jung's view on the purpose of alchemy. Edinger, Edward F. (1984), p. 87, Edinger notes: "The psyche is all found on the outside...because the outside and the unconscious are effectively the same thing."

456 Radin, D. I., & Rebman, J. M. (1996). Are phantasms fact or fantasy? A preliminary investigation of apparitions evoked in the laboratory. *Journal-Society for Psychical Research, 61*, 65–87.

457 Moody, R. A. (1992), p. 111.

458 Moody, R. A. (1992), p. 113.

459 Roll, W. G. (2004), p. 257.

460 Evans-Wentz, W. Y. (1958), p. 211.

461 Mills, A., Haraldsson, E., & Keil, H. J. (1994), p. 207.

462 Mills, A., Haraldsson, E., & Keil, H. J. (1994), p. 217.

463 Not all Buddhist sects reject the idea of an eternal Self.

464 Shin, K. (2013), p. 79.

465 Parfit, D. (1995), p. 14.

466 Parfit, D. (1995), p. 16.

467 Maung, H. H. (2007). *Consciousness: An Enquiry into the Metaphysics of the Self.* Lulu Press, p. 151.

468 Kastrup, B. (2020).

469 James, W. (1890), Vol 1, p. 292.

470 Colman, A. M. (2001). *A Dictionary of Psychology.* Oxford University Press, p. 239.

471 Von Franz, M. L. (1999), p. 294. Von Franz describes Jung's view of the Self as that which governs the psyche; the ego is within the psyche.

472 Ludden, David (2020). https://www.psychologytoday.com/us/blog/talking-apes/202004/what-remains-the-self-after-memory-is-gone. Accessed May 17, 2020.

473 Ram-Prasad, C. (2013), pp. 53–54.

474 Fasching, W. (2011). Phenomenological Reflections on the Indian Notion of Witness-Consciousness. *Self, No Self?: Perspectives from Analytical, Phenomenological, and Indian Traditions*, p. 197.

475 Ram-Prasad, C. (2013), p. 60.

476 Ram-Prasad, C. (2013), p. 61.

477 Ram-Prasad, C. (2013), p. 61.

478 Schwerin, A., (2007). Schwerin argues that "Hume's rejection of a rival view of the self is flawed in that it commits the fallacy of equivocation: a serious shortcoming that undermines Hume's arguments for his own view on the self" (15–16).

479 Shin, K. (2013), p. 85.

480 Dreyfus, Georges, (2010), p. 116. Dunlap, K. (1914), p. 66. In this early paper, Dunlap states: "I am not at present interested in delimiting the Self; I do not know that it is possible to show where the Self leaves off and the non-Self begins.

I am merely interested in identifying the concrete basis, or I might say, the core of the Self." This 'core' of the Self is what I have termed the 'egoless I'.

481 Harvey, P. (1993), p. 30.

482 Lama, D. (2002), p. 119.

483 Lama, D. (2005). p. 128.

484 Carroll, Sean and Alan Wallace. (2017).

485 Neale, M. (2009), p. 48. The Buddha was against the idea of "nihilism" or terminal fate.

486 Rudd, A. (2015), p. 883.

487 Evans-Wentz, W. Y. (1968), pp. lviii, xxxix. Jung, in his Psychological Commentary to *The Tibetan Book of the Great Liberation* states: "It is interesting to note that in the East, too, there are 'heretics' who identify the Self with the ego. With us this heresy is pretty widespread and is subscribed to by all those who firmly believe that ego-consciousness is the only form of psychic life." Von Franz, M. L. (1998), p. 117. Von Franz notes that there is a deeper consciousness that belongs to the Self, and that exists partly out of space and time. She avers, "It is therefore that part of man which survives death." Jung, C. G. (1960), p. 224. Jung explains how the ego weakens when there is an afflux of "unconscious contents," resulting in a "new totality-figure I call the *self*"; confirmation that to Jung, the ego and the self are not one and the same.

488 Albahari, M. (2002), p. 7.

489 Albahari, M. (2011), p. 80.

490 Albahari, M. (2011), p. 80.

491 Albahari, M. (2011), p. 89.

492 Albahari, M. (2011), p. 93.

493 Huxley, Aldous. (1990), p. 35.

494 Lescarboura, A. C. (1920), p. 446.

495 Bostrom, N. (2003), pp. 243–255.

496 Smith, H. (1991), p. 388.

Index

Made in the USA
Middletown, DE
19 November 2021

52944278R00161